Come traveling with June

Shandal Publishing, Saint-Petersburg, Russia

COME TRAVELING WITH JUNE

Published by Shandal Publishing,
P.O. Box 614, St. Petersburg, 197198, Russia
e-mail: julia@shandal.ru

Designed by Zhury Svetlana

Dr. June M. Temple
C325 1909 Salton Rd.
Abbotsford, BC V2S 5B6
e-mail: jmt@rapidnet.net

ISBN: 5-93925-065-3

Printed in Russia

CONTENTS

*With Thankfulness in my heart
to my brothers in Christ,
Gene Parkins and Win Wachsmann,
for the hours they have spent
to make the publication
of Come Travelling With June possible.*

PREFACE

Some people would claim I was born on some type of moving vehicle. This is not true, I was born in a perfectly good hospital. It is true I traveled a great deal from the time I was a tiny baby.

During the years when most people did not travel far from their home my family visited relatives in neighboring states. Then even as far as 1200 miles away from home and finally all the way from the east coast to the west coast of the United States.

Chuck, the man I married, came from a family who never traveled further than 60 miles from home. But he was bitten by the vagabond bug and enjoyed traveling a much as I did.

Now as a Mission Representative, a teacher and speaker, plus having children and grandchildren living in different locations my days are still filled with travel.

The story of a good part my life and of the many travels enjoyed can be found in five books.

BUSH TEACHER SERIES
1. GROWING IN HIS LIGHT (childhood)
2. THROUGH PASTURES AND VALLEYS (young adult)
3. BUSH TEACHER IN B.C.
4. BUSH TEACHER II
5. OPENED DOORS

Some of the following stories have appeared in Christian magazines. A few are excerpts (rewritten as short stories) from other books written by Dr. June M. Temple. Many of the stories have never been published.

DEADLY BEAUTY

The two week camping trip was over. Our family of six spent time each day enjoying all the activities and now the 5:30 a.m. ringing of our pocket-sized alarm brought us to the reality of packing for the day's drive home.

Fawn, the family dog, was secured to the picnic table. Suddenly Pauline, who glanced out of the tent window said, "Daddy, there's a snake headed for Fawn, and he's whimpering."

Daddy armed himself with a rolled sleeping bag, and headed out the door to protect the

family pet. Behind him were our sons Charles and David. Their father threw the sleeping bag in front of the snake thinking it would deter the reptile, but the creature started crawling over the bag.

The boys watched their dad lift one end of the bed roll and flip the snake. It slithered off in another direction.

Then David said "Daddy, that snake is just like the one the lifeguard kept for a pet. Let's catch him." Soon the three males were by the beautifully marked serpent. The head of our house put his foot upon the head of the snake to hold it still. The serpent's head turned in order to sink its fangs into the shoe's sole.

Fortunately the fangs missed the foot. Then the boys' dad reached down and picked the reptile up at the point where the back of its head joined the body.

The three foot snake's body was quite thick and its copper, gold, and brown colored head glistened in the morning sun. This wriggling, writhing form actually caught itself into a knot as it was carried to the tent for my two daughters and myself to view. With its strong flailing body it unwound itself, and with each movement made itself more difficult to hold.

A neighboring campers voice said, "Man, that's a copperhead!" With that remark the snake was thrown into a close-by water trough. The copperhead slithered over the narrow side of the trough, and fell to the ground. People who were gathered around now scattered, and from all directions could be heard "Kill him! Get a hatchet! Get a shovel! Stay away!

There was no sympathy for this lethal creature. The snake's head was properly smashed with a shovel, severed with a hatchet, and buried in the ground.

A copperhead snake is beautiful to behold. However its appearance is deceiving. How many things in life are like that?

For years cigarette smoking, heavy drinking and drugs have been considered bad habits, yet the pleasure outweighed any ugly connotation associated with it. Today we know such "bad habits" have become a death warrant for many.

It appears such habits are copperhead snakes ensnaring people in the physical realm. Is it possible there could also be the same type of serpent in the moral realm? Immediately the HIV virus, and abortion come into mind. But these, once again, bring about a physical death.

What I have in mind is the death of a moral conscience.

Many of the people who produce what is watched by young and old on TV and in theaters today are insidiously teaching their own lack of morals. Sex, foul language and violence has definitely become very much a part of every day life. Even Christian young people take the attitude everyone is doing it so why shouldn't I. Apparently there is such a thing as moral death.

One more diabolical serpent rears its ugly head in preparation to strike. This one is in the Spiritual realm. The deceitfulness of modern philosophies seem so right. Mankind offers all kinds of excuses rather than accepting God's plan for Salvation.

We hear "I'm not so bad or I've enough "brownie points" to get into heaven." Or we hear the opposite "I've been so bad God will never forgive me." Then there is the argument "It doesn't matter what you believe as long as you believe there is a God." One more concept, that of the New Age movement, is "Everyone is a God." Continuously excuses abound! They all seem so much more rational than the simple solution offered by God Himself.

The only absolute truth is that God loves us. The Creator loves us so much He sent His only Son to die for us. The Son died to pay our debt of sin. Our only requirement is to ask God's forgiveness for our sins, and to ask Jesus to be our Saviour. The Lord Jesus Christ, God's Son longs for us to come to Him.

Something so simple seems deceiving, but in reality all other philosophies are the deceptive ones. Oh, that mankind would not be so deceived! Spiritual death is endless.

GO TO THE CROSS

Pungent odors wafted around Olivera Street, the Mexican section of Los Angeles. Chuck said "Look at that handiwork," and we stopped at the stall holding tooled leather purses, and belts. In the back of the stall there was a man working and we stood fascinated while watching him pound patterns into the leather. Minutes passed as we gazed.

Then our son David, (with whom we were vacationing) along with his wife, and their tiny baby Joshua led the way to the next booth. The display of straw baskets, hats and purses caught our eyes. We stopped to peer at all the items, and chatted about the work entailed. Again a craftsman was working before our eyes. This one was intricately weaving straw, and we stood mesmerized.

There were booths of silver jewelry; rings, pins, necklaces, and earrings. Booths of embroidered clothing; blouses, shirts, and dresses. Booths of artwork; oil, and water- colors on canvas or velvet. Booth after booth of these items, and in-between them the booths with the cooking items simmering. The smell of the meat for Tacos, Burritos, and Fajitas tickled our nostrils. There were people munching everywhere as the noon hour approached.

To the side of each food stall stood a rack, or an enclosed container of interesting looking pastries. They were long, thin, and sugar coated. Arnette (David's wife) said "They're called Churros, and they're good." Chuck and I decided to be daring enough to try the new item. Our taste-buds were made merry by the delicious sweet donut-like dough. We too joined the munching crowds.

A rumor began to catch our ears as it was passed over and over among the people walking around us, or standing by the stalls. It was about the filming of a very popular TV program. We heard a scene would be shot right at this place at any minute. When we saw everyone moving toward the entrance of the Mexican street we followed, and joined the crowd to watch the cameramen setup; Many people lined both sides of the walkway.

First the cameraman shot scenes with the extra actors he brought with him. Then he swung the camera toward a large cross at the market's entryway, and finally toward the curb where a yellow taxi pulled-up and stopped. Out stepped a well known actor who started walking up the path to the shopping area. As he was walking the director kept saying, "Go to the cross." It seemed the actor was deep in thought, and did not hear the director. The people in the crowd started murmuring "Go to the cross." Louder and louder the murmur rose until all were shouting "Go to the cross."

The actor never walked to the beautiful stone cross standing in the middle of the path. It seemed almost impossible for anyone to miss.

The director yelled "Cut," and moved everyone toward a different area of the street to shoot a different scene.

Months later we were visiting in another home when the TV was turned on. Before our eyes we saw the program we watched being filmed. It opened with the actor walking to the cross. There he met another individual. The refilming of the scene must have been exceedingly costly, as is everything within the filming industry.

In the center of history stands another cross, a wooden one. The Son of God died on it to save mankind. The Bible tells us in John 19:16b-18a "So they took Jesus and led Him away. And He, bearing His cross, went out to a place called the Place of a Skull, which is called in Hebrew, Golgotha, where they crucified Him," In the Bible we are told "For Christ also suffered once for sins, the just for the unjust, that He might bring us to God, being put to death in the flesh but made alive by the Spirit."

The only assumption to draw from these verses is every human being must make the journey to the wooden cross, and meet the person of Jesus Christ. If an individual does not realize Jesus Christ died to give them the gift of Salvation the result will be very costly. More costly than the refilming of a movie scene. A cost for all eternity. Forever to be separated from God.

As the four of us watched the filming we thought "everyone is yelling the Christian message. The gift of life is being proclaimed, yet, as in the case of the actor it's being missed, never even heard. How like life!"

PLEASE COME BACK

The thermometer registered 45 degrees below zero. My husband Chuck and I were undressing in an unheated house of a missionary compound in order to crawl between icy sheets for a night's rest. Our shivering bodies and chattering teeth lasted for about 20 minutes before the radiating warmth of a five inch down comforter permeated us.

Before dropping off to sleep we chatted about the day being spent in driving miles through barren country. Most of the time our car slowly jiggled and bumped over a snow packed gravel road. This night we were sleeping close to a reserve in central British Columbia and the closest town was 112 miles away.

Our purpose for traveling the distance was to bring a Gospel team from a Native Bible School to the village of Chilenko Forks in order for the students to be involved a few days with a missionary couple. Two busy days were planned for the young people's team made up of Gloria, Rose and Art.

After a good night's rest the three Native young people looked forward to an after- noon of door to door visitation on the Reserve. Then in the evening the Reserve young people were invited to the missionaries home for fellowship and an ice cream social.

Us four missionaries Ralph, Wanda, Chuck and myself spent time churning ice cream the old fashioned way, and then found out none of the Chilenko Forks young people liked it. Once they tasted the smooth creamy cold vanilla flavor they said, "It's too sweet."

We didn't know it, but to the native people in this area ice cream was a concoction made from very bitter berries. The berry is whipped until its pink froth looks like meringue. Then some sugar is added, but the bitterness completely covers any sugar sweetness.

Their taste buds could not accept what white man called ice cream. Despite the cultural blunder the young people enjoyed a good time together.

On the second day Ralph, Chuck and Art planned to fly to a remote, isolated cabin to visit with an Indian family. Wanda, Rose and Gloria decided to again visit the reserve in order to be involved with the women who lived there.

Once more the actual contacts were planned for the afternoon and evening. While we made the ice cream blunder, we did know the fact about visiting a reserve before noon was not an accepted practice in Indian culture.

My contribution was to stay with Ralph and Wanda's small children. This would allow Wanda to be free to go with the team girls to visit in homes.

Ralph checked the skis on his plane, the oil, the gas, the cockpit run down, and any other item necessary before taking off in the bitter cold. None of the men wanted to be stranded in the remote area to which they were traveling.

The takeoff went smoothly. Even though there was no heat in the cockpit where the three men sat they did not mind, because of being filled with the anticipation of visiting the isolated family. The plane flew over tree tops and frozen lakes before catching sight of the cabin's smoke.

Ralph zoomed over the cabin itself, then headed for a lake (about a mile further) on which to land. First Ralph circled the lake before making his approach. Then he asked,

"Do you see any overflow?" Neither Chuck nor Art were exactly sure what the appearance of overflow looked like. They all gave a searching look over the lake. Because no one saw anything unusual Ralph landed the plane. Chuck and Art jumped out of the cockpit into knee deep slush. Then they knew something was unusual. It was overflow.

The phenomenon of overflow is peculiar to northern lakes. Thick ice sinks a little into the water, which then flows over the top of the ice. Snow falls until some of it becomes slush and more snow sits on top of the slush to give the false appearance of just snow. This produces a very dangerous condition on which to land a plane. The plane's skies immediately freeze into the slush, and become firmly stuck there.

Ralph knew he was in trouble. He told Chuck he would need to take off right away and gunned the engines, but the plane would not budge. Then Ralph called, "You two wiggle the tail of the plane while I gun the engines." Chuck and Art wiggled. Nothing happened. Again and again they wiggled. All of this time they were standing in knee- deep slush, which trickled down inside their mucklucks. Even though their coats were warm they felt like they were standing naked behind the plane's engine blast. Who knew the wind chill factor the prop blew; minus 75, minus 125? Still with all of the wiggling nothing happened. The men began to envision themselves isolated with the Indian family until spring breakup.

Ralph leaned out the cockpit window and yelled, "Let's try something different. You men lift the tail, while I gun the engine." Art and Chuck strained and pushed-up. The plane broke loose and shot like a bullet across the lake. When Ralph stopped on good firm ice (a half mile from the men) he leaned out the window and waved for Chuck and Art to join him. The two males were heavily panting by the time they finished the laborious run through the slush. Ralph said, "Hop in, we can't stay here."

As Ralph circled the lake to head for home the men saw a horse drawn sleigh moving down the path to the lake. The Native family was coming to take their visitors back to the cabin. Everyone in the wagon was waving as if to say please come back, please come back.

Ralph murmured "They will never understand why we didn't stay. They will think they did something to offend us."

The gospel team trip was over. Each one of us held some special memory of the time of ministry. However Chuck's memory was the most poignant. To him, the native family waving for the three men to come back vividly etched into his mind the picture of lost mankind pleading for someone to come tell them about God's plan of Salvation. Chuck thought about how Art would have enjoyed telling this Native family about the way he found Christ out on a Reserve in the Yukon, and about the change in his life. Chuck pictured the lonely faces, the waving arms, the pleading "Please come back" as a living portrayal of the Bible verses "For whoever calls upon the name of the Lord shall be saved. How then shall they call on Him in whom they have not believed? And how shall they believe in Him of whom they have not heard? And how shall they hear without someone to tell them?"

ON THE BEACH

Fluffy white clouds glided across the vividly blue sky. My eyes watched with rapt attention as figures formed in the clouds; fishes and poodles and angels took shape.

My eyes now were diverted to the glistening sunshine on the water and the tiny waves lapping at the shore. Creatures teemed in the mud of the low tide. I watched parents pointing out the tiny sea life to their children.

All of the awesome beauty brought tears to my eyes. Now the need filled me to talk to my Almighty Creator. To thank the One who loves me and to Praise Him for the beauty around me. To chat about the joys and heartaches in my life. To give to my Lord the grief of loneliness because now my life partner was in the presence of God.

A great peace from the King of Kings surrounded me. It filled me with joy and a verse from one of the psalms came to my mind. "Great peace have those who love Your law, And nothing causes them to stumble."

ANGELS ???

"There's been an accident" rang in my ears and I woke with a start. My heart pounded a mile a minute because the voice I heard in my dream was that of my deceased husband. Immediately every possible type of accident which could happen to my children and grandchildren while they were at home, in a car, at work, at school, in an airplane began to fill my mind. I actually started to become nauseated and then told myself, "it's only a dream, don't dwell on it." However I couldn't shake the feeling and for all of the day a fear clenched my heart every time the phone rang.

My car began to shimmy in the front end and I thought, "It probably needs an alignment from a pot hole I hit a couple of weeks ago." Each day the shimmy was a little worse and I began to wonder if I should take the car in for an alignment before my 150 mile trip south, or if the work could wait until I returned. The night before my departure, while I was driving on a freeway, the shimmy was so terrible I couldn't travel the speed limit. Now I was sure the problem couldn't wait.

Early the next morning I drove the car to a shop where the attendant took the vehicle out for a check ride. He found both front tires contained a huge balloon bubble in them. New tires were purchased, and while they were being put on the attendant found a broken seal which also was replaced. Three hours later I started my trip feeling safe. While driving

I wondered if the dream was really a warning for my safety. A blowout at 65 miles an hour is a pretty frightening thought.

On my return trip I was traveling 65 miles an hour in the left hand lane. Slightly in front of me and in the center lane was a huge semi-truck. The same distance at my rear in the center lane, was a car. Suddenly the semi jerked into my lane and as I began to see black marks appearing on the road in front of me the idea popped into my head, "He's jammed on the brakes."

There was no shoulder as we were on the approach to a small bridge. My choice was to play "kamikaze pilot" into the back of the truck, or floor the gas pedal and dart in front of the car at my rear. I chose the latter. Once in the middle lane my vision caught the sight of a huge pipe across the middle and right lanes. It was located just 20 feet in front of me.

When I was in back of the middle-lane semi, the rig's height blocked all view of what was taking place to the right of him. The truck driver saw the pipe fall from a truck and that was when he pulled in front of me.

There was nothing for me to do but jam on the brakes. I felt the car lift and then stop when it hit the pipe. The sensation was like the front wheels traveled over the monster pipe, and it was jammed somewhere under the car.

I was not hurt. Not one scratch. Not one bruise. All the other cars were stopped in back of me and the people's eyes were riveted on me to see if I could move.

I stepped out of the car to find where the pipe was located. There it sat with the front end of the car resting on top. "Would the pipe budge if it was kicked?" entered my mind. So I kicked it and out it popped. On inspecting the front end of the car there wasn't a scratch or a dent. It appeared to be a miraculous accident.

The truck driver walked over and rolled the pipe to the side of the road. I assured everyone I was fine, even though I felt shaky. Then we were all on our way once again.

"There was an accident," just as the voice in my dream said. However there must have been angels placed on each side of the front end of my car who gently lifted it and placed it on the pipe. There must have also been an air-bag of angels around me in the car. How else can such a bizarre accident with no injuries, or car damage, be explained?

AUSTRALIA

Once you've been there you want to return!

Traveling to the land down under never called to me. Seeing the film "Crocodile Dundee," while enjoyable, did nothing to pique my interest. Yet that is precisely where I visited. You see I offered my grandson Patrick a trip of his choice for a College graduation present. He chose Australia, and I found myself having a ball there.

Patrick's college friend spent the previous summer in Australia and advised my grandson about all the places to see and things to do. When Patrick told his friend he was going to be in Sydney for four days and Brisbane for four days his friend said "It's impossible to see and do everything in four days." Patrick took-up the challenge and we did prove his friend wrong.

Flying for 13 hours with a 15 hour time change is a cataclysmic event. We landed in Sydney at 6 a.m. to be "off and running" (as soon as our feet hit the ground) for 12 straight hours. By the time I collapsed in bed I had been awake for 40 hours and I never did adjust to the time change. However my sleeplessness didn't effect our daily schedule. Patrick experienced no problem adjusting to Australian time.

Let me say now, Australia is a land of pleasant, helpful people. The lodging accommodations are clean, spacious and reasonably priced. Restaurant prices are comparable to North

American ones, with choices from McDonald's, Kentucky Fried Chicken to those of the most elegant. Best of all there is very little difference in the dollar's exchange rate.

The beauty of Sydney with its magnificent harbor rivals the beauty of Vancouver, British Columbia. The city itself is built on eleven islands as well as on the mainland. Three of the islands are now connected by bridges and the other eight can easily be reached by short ferry rides of 10 to 30 minutes.

Patrick and I found three of the islands of unique interest. Located on Manley Island is a huge aquarium. There Patrick and I walked on the harbor floor while encircled in glass. We watched schools of multi-colored fish, we walked beside sharks and underneath stingrays, plus a multitude of other sea creatures. The two of us were fortunate to be there at feeding time and it was quite a sight to see two young women divers hand-feed twelve foot long sharks and three foot wide stingrays along with all of the other fish.

Manley itself is a picturesque island with lovely shops and restaurants bordering the bay's waterfront. We ate lunch at one of the picnic tables facing the water and both of us ordered fish and chips. The name of the fish was one we never heard before, yet it was a delicious flaky white meat.

The Ocean side of Manley Island is within walking distance of the harbor. We took the trek to view a lovely white beach full of people enjoying sun and sand. The water looked inviting and there were people swimming, jumping breakers and just splashing around. Swimming areas are protected against shark attack. Although such a thing is rare now days, and the Australians stress how many years it has been since a shark attack occurred, the risk is there and it's a sobering thought.

Our return trip to the mainland was on a vessel called a "River Cat," (a catamaran). Both regular ferries and "The Cat" are available to ride to the islands, the latter reduced the travel time in half. Having traveled to the island on one and back on the other we could say both rides were enjoyable.

Day two's main attraction for us was the Toronga Park Zoo. Once more the use of a ferry became necessary to travel to this exceptional park built on the side of a cliff. Close to where the ferry docked a bus service was available to travel to the top area of the zoo, or else a tram could be ridden up. We chose the excitement of the tram.

Every type of animal imaginable is housed on this cliff side; from common to exotic, from endangered to abundant, from crawling, to flying to swimming. We spent hours looking and watching while slowly strolling down one descending path after another toward the harbor.

Of particular interest to us was the display of Koala bears. The little creatures were sleeping in five to six foot high trees. We could stand right next to them and have our picture taken while being told facts about the Koala bears by park guards. Can you imagine sleeping for 20 hours? They do. We saw the Ostrich, the Kangaroo and the Wallaby, thinking all along about the sense of humor God had when he made the animals peculiar to Australia.

When Patrick and I almost reached the bottom of the Cliff we heard an announcement over the loudspeaker about a seal show in the aqua center section of the zoo. We watched a seal show the day before at the Aquarium, but didn't want to miss this one, so we huffed and puffed up the cliff side to the Aqua Center. The show was worth the hike. Although it was much the same in content as the day before, here there were instructions as to the teaching techniques used to command each seal's actions.

Day three in Sydney took us by ferry to Darling Harbor where the huge Marine Museum is located. This month their feature was on whales and the knowledge given was very

23

extensive, with what was told was also being shown through the whale reproductions on the floor of the museum.

Close to the museum sat a large shopping center. There we ate lunch in the food court, and browsed through some of the shops before sailing back to the mainland.

All of the ferries dock in an area called Central Quay; a unique setting with an extensive promenade and walkway from the Sydney Opera House on the East to the historical area on the West known as "The Rocks."

In-between our trips by ferry we explored the shops and restaurants along this passageway. A few Aborigines thrummed their degiree-doos, or danced at different locations along the harbor. From time to time a juggler, or a musician, or a magician, or a person miming performed on the promenade. People thronged the area.

Patrick and I visited the Opera House and walked through the Royal Botanic Gardens next to it. We strolled along the parkway back to "The Rocks" where the first ships landed in Australia. Then on to tour the museum and quaint shops. In three days we felt we touched most of the major Sydney sights.

One big asset enabling us to do so much was a five-day bus pass. This little two inch by three inch piece of plastic coated paper enabled us to travel on any bus or ferry (without cost) plus three Sydney harbor cruises of three hours each. On Friday evening we enjoyed the lovely city lights harbor cruise. The second one, the River cruise was scheduled for Sunday morning, our last day in this city.

With Sunday well planned we started out at nine a.m. The cruise was interesting. While on it we saw a huge open-air market in "The Rocks" area and learned the sale was a usual Sunday occurrence. As soon as the boat docked we went to the market to browse for a couple of hours before joining the mobs of people walking toward the Opera House.

Sydney is a city of over three million people, of whom two hundred thousand are of Greek decent. It seemed all two hundred thousand of them were in the Opera House area. This March day was the Greek Independence Day from the rule of the Ottoman Empire; brought about by a battle fought in 1821. They celebrated the day in a big way!

Located on one side of the square sat a large platform, before which were many occupied seats. Every inch of the multitude of steps up to the Opera House was crammed with a mass of people.

The festivities began with a parade across the space between the chairs and the platform; Bands, Lodges, Clubs, School children, Bagpipers, and Dignitaries all marched. The speeches from City officials and Greek Orthodox Church and School dignitaries started after the parade. Finally, what we were especially interested in, the Greek Dancing began. There were dances for men, dances for women and mixed dancing; dancing by dancing classes, dances by schools and dances by clubs. For Patrick and myself the afternoon proved full of interesting Greek culture and history. A fine finale for our Sydney stay.

Early the next morning we were off to the airport for a two hour flight to Brisbane. Our first day in this city went bye like a whirlwind. This section of our tour included a bus trip for each day.

First we traveled up the Sunshine Coast through lush Pineapple Crops, Sugar Cane Crops and lovely gardens of all kinds. The bus made two stops at Plantations for us to view the work going on there. Then on we traveled to our lunch destination at the seaside resort town of Noosa; a picturesque village just beyond the Dream Mountains. After a walk on the beach we stopped in a tiny Mall for lunch. I asked the waitress for a sandwich and Root Beer. She never heard of such a beverage and told me their soft drinks were "Coke,

Sprite and Ginger Root Beer. I tried the latter to find my taste buds did not appreciate the flavor.

Ginger grows in great profusion in Australia and is used in many of their dishes. At one of the plantations I ate a ginger muffin and thoroughly enjoyed it. But as a beverage someone else can have Ginger Root Beer as far as I was concerned. Patrick finished my drink.

Two candy bars were recommended to my by my co-worker, Betty Kirsch, who grew-up in the "Land Down Under." Patrick and I searched diligently for Violet Crumble and Polly Waffle. When we found them we purchased one of each. The Polly Waffle definitely was our preferred one. It was made of marshmallow cream encased in a waffle-like cone and dipped in milk chocolate. First I thought I'd just eat half of the bar and save the other half for another day. Within five minutes I gave-up and consumed the other half. It's good I don't live in Australia or very shortly none of my clothes would fit.

Violet Crumble is thinly spun sugar with a slight molasses flavor. The mass looks like a very miniature honey comb dipped in chocolate and very sweet to the taste.

Day two tour took us down the gold coast where we got off the bus in the ocean front town of Surfers Paradise. Beside the beach and the pounding surf the town was filled with many shops. We went in one after another looking for gifts for our families back home. Our quest was successful and we entered the bus with arms full of packages.

For our final day in Brisbane the two of us took the city tour and a harbor cruise. Heat seemed intense in this city. The bus was air-conditioned, the ship was air-conditioned, our hotel was air- conditioned, but walking on the street felt like we were underneath an electric blanket with the dial turned on high. Still we persisted because we didn't want to miss any sights.

All too soon the last day of our time in Australia drew to a close. There is no doubt the whirlwind experience was one we'll never forget. Early the next morning we flew back to Sydney to catch the plane home. Patrick held a regular coach fare ticket. I traveled stand-bye. Low and behold there was no room on the flight for grandmom. I waved good-bye to Patrick and ended-up spending two more days in Sydney on my own. No problem! I relaxed from eight days of running, and also took the third harbor cruise we did not have time to do together.

The cruise is one forever etched in my mind. As the ship sailed by one of the beaches, the captain announced "And on the right is our nude beach." At the far and of the beach was a clump of rocks extending into the water. We were quite close and as we passed the rocky point a very large naked man with a huge belly stood up and waved to us. Up to this point all of the passengers were attempting to be dignified with the sight before us, but when the man waved everyone broke out laughing. The ship rocked with laughter

The trip I did not particularly desire to take became a wonderful one, and I now enjoy the memories. Memories of all the beauty and the unusual creatures God made for us to enjoy in that part of the world, plus memories of a wonderful fun time with a grown grandson. I'm also ready to return to Australia.

HONG KONG BOUND

People exclaim, "You went to Hong Kong!" Yes, let me tell you how such a trip was made possible. In May it was my pleasure to meet Anita Post, a young Chinese woman who grew up in Hong Kong and now lived in Kentucky. I mentioned to her the fact of visiting China was a secret desire of mine. Anita said, "You should come while I am there."

The concept sounded great, but because of finances, such a trip could only be a "pipe dream." I put the idea on a back burner in my mind, but it kept surfacing and I would catch myself thinking, what an opportunity, or, Communist takeover of the city takes place shortly and I should go before it happens. Still such a trip was beyond my means. Finally I prayed, "God, if you want me to go there please send me an unexpected check in today's mail."

Believe it or not when I went to the mail box it contained just such a check. It was a refund from my car insurance company (for a car I previously owned). The check was only $40. But then, I hadn't asked for a large check and the next day I made my reservations to travel.

Within two weeks six unexpected checks arrived totaling almost the entire cost of the trip. I stood in amazement over the never thought possible refunds and rebates appearing in the mail.

The scheduled flight route was from Seattle to San Francisco to Hong Kong; the latter segment being fifteen hours of straight flying time. Whenever I mentioned this fact there almost always followed another repetitive statement "What does a person do all that time on a plane." I respond, "Well, there are usually two movies offered, and of course two meals, plus the snacks (all of which take some time). Then I carry on board a word puzzle book, reading material and some small piece of embroidery to occupy more time. All of the latter is pleasant to do while also listening to music on the head set.

Sleep is another option for some people, but not one I'm too successful with. Although on this flight I was fortunate enough to have an empty seat next to mine and I could lay down. I managed to succeed in taking two naps of about two hours each.

Approaching the Hong Kong airport the view was spectacular as the plane flew over lovely lush islands and across blue water. The runway approach was bordered with attractive high-rise apartment complexes on one side and within my eyesight on the right lay the sparkling bay with majestic Hong Kong island's business section in the distance.

At 5:15 p.m. the plane's passenger door opened and a mass of people, including myself, flowed into the airport. There a surprise waited for me as neither Anita Post nor her husband CA could been seen. It appeared I was on my own, so I hailed a cab and gave the driver the brochure with the hotel address on it. He said "I no read English."

My next step was to try to pronounce the address. He finally understood and off we went. Surprise number two came when he said the fare cost $175.00. There was nothing I could do but pay him.

Then surprise number three was right around the corner. The reservation at the hotel was mistakenly scheduled for the next day. They did not have an empty room, but offered to fix the sitting room of an occupied suite for me for $800. I didn't think I was ready for that. So I obtained some change to use the phone to call Anita. She came right over to get me and took me to where she and her husband CA were staying in a condo.

By the time I arrived at Anita and CA's home it was almost 10 p.m. and I had been up for twenty-seven hours. As far as I was concerned the bed was the most inviting article of furniture in her suite..

Six-thirty the next morning my eyes flew open and I was ready to go see and do anything and everything. An hour later the three of us walked to a park to watch CA take his Tai-Chi class.

The park appeared busy with people walking or jogging, plus others playing basketball and doing all kinds of exercises. The Tai Chi teacher, with eight women and CA (the only male) began the ancient exercise warm-up. There are forty-eight distinct moves to the whole exercise, of which CA learned three-fourths of the number during his four weeks in Hong Kong. Most of the class members already knew all of the moves and they were there just for their daily work out.

Hunger's call took us to a small restaurant after class. The first taste of food actually made in China passed my lips. A variety of dishes were ordered and divided between the three of us.

Tepid tea, in a glass was served to our table as soon as we were seated. I enjoyed drinking a large glass of fresh squeezed orange juice. Then came ham and scrambled eggs between two slices of crustless, untoasted bread and followed with a type of French toast. This well-known American dish was very un-American with a thin layer of peanut butter spread between the two pieces of white bread before it was dipped and cooked as one unit. Syrup was served on the side. Lastly three types of sweet buns were shared. Breakfast was yummy!

Food did not have a chance to settle before we were off to travel on the underground (subway) and then take a train to the Chinese University of Hong Kong where Anita was Professor-on-loan for the summer. CA kept contact with his work in the Medical Research Center at the University of Kentucky through the computer in Anita's office.

When their business in the office was partly completed a break was taken in order for us to have a relaxing swim in the University's Olympic sized swimming pool. Later lunch followed in the University's Teachers dining area with other Professors and guests from Anita's department.

Chopsticks were the common table utensil and a new learning experience for me. I adopted a "sink or swim" attitude about them. It was possible to keep my head above water and to get some food into my mouth.

One Professor ordered a variety of fish, chicken and rice dishes for everyone. Here began my amazement over the amount of food these Chinese people could consume, yet they weren't an obese people.

There were new tastes for my palate, new combinations of foods and a new concept of how to manage chicken with bone fragments, bony fish and a dish held under my chin from which I shoveled rice into my mouth. I learned some food was enjoyable while other dishes were tolerable and some were just to be endured.

The uniqueness of the University site on the side of a mountain caught my attention when we left Anita's office to meander down toward the train. New modern buildings stood out among the green tropical trees, bushes and flowers. Paths wound either up or down through this growth. On one of the paths there was even a tiny bridge across a little stream and a small waterfall could be seen to the right. Everywhere the highest technology or newest learning process could be identified. The Chinese University of Hong Kong was truly a credit to this country.

Now we were mingling with rush hour traffic. Masses and masses of humanity going through turnstiles into the train area. The entire underground tunnels became wave after wave of undulating movement. Platforms contained walls of people, fifteen bodies thick to cram into the cars. Despite the volume of people our travel time did not take any longer than the morning trip to the University.

I checked into my hotel room and we scheduled dinner to be held in a Chiu Chau restaurant. This name came from a Province of China which is distinct for the way they prepared their food. It was unusual.

Anita and CA wanted to completely immerse me into the culinary culture of this country. My taste buds were now introduced to eel, goose, and jellyfish. Several times in the states I was served goose, but the preparation of this one was especially tasty. While on the other hand the jellyfish texture was like slimy rubber bands and the flavor was tasteless. Many slivers of chicken were among the slimy rubber bands. This was the only thing which gave the dish any taste. The eel was cooked whole and then chopped into chunks, bone, skin and meat. The taste was slightly oily and very bland.

Sightseeing began the next morning after Anita and CA arrived at the hotel. Our goal this day was to use the moving stairway up the side of one of Hong Kong's streets. This upward flow extended for several kilometers to a halfway point up to Victoria Peak

Anita asked, "How far do you want to ride" and my answer was, "The whole way." She countered, "You know there is no down escalator." To my way of thinking any walking down a hill or down stairs presented no problem.

The view from the bottom looked like a stairway extending to heaven. Located at the very base was a moving walkway where we needed to hold the railing tightly because the angle was very steep. There were several of these walkways. Then the moving stairs began.

Slowly we progressed up and up. Sometimes by the motorized means and other times by walking on overpasses above streets to reach the next escalator.

Our view, in all directions from the top of the stairs, was excellent. Next began the descent; step after step, flat area after flat area and on and on and on. By now the heat and humidity was becoming very oppressive. About two-thirds of the way down we stepped into an air conditioned shop to cool off, browse and rest.

The store contained beautiful pieces of jade, carved wood, pottery and oil paintings. We must have spent half an hour looking at the variety of exquisitely hand made objects. By now we were cooled, rested and hungry.

From this point we moved a block away to Pottinger Street, to continue our decent. This street did not contain any moving sidewalks, but consisted entirely of steps. Lining both side of the stairs were tiny stalls containing various goods for sale. About nine feet of open steps existed between the stalls. There was no railing. Just step after step. An interesting place for browsing, but an area where quality was questionable and much bargaining was necessary to reach a reasonable purchase price.

We ate lunch in a charming Japanese Restaurant and feasted this time on a variety of foods authentic to the northern island nation. The food content was much like the Chinese menu. However, due to its preparation entirely different in taste and also quite delicious.

CA and I were on our own for the afternoon as Anita needed to take care of some work at the University. He took me to one shopping center after another. Some were in order to shop for gifts to take home. Others just to observe their uniqueness.

While we were down town I saw two newly constructed banking complexes which were of a most interesting architectural construction. The Shanghai bank of Hong Kong appeared to be built like a battleship, including canons on its roof. The comical thing was from certain angles it appeared the guns were pointed at the newer beautiful Bank of China. This latter high-rise greatly towered over any of the other high-rises.

On boarding a ferry from Hong Kong for Kowloon's shopping area we watched the downtown island slip away as the ferry's wake rippled. Less expensive shopping was available in Kowloon and I was able to purchase several gifts.

As we were ready to leave Kowloon to return to my hotel we noticed warning flags were posted to alert people of a coming Typhoon. CA advised me the next day's activities would depend on how severely the Typhoon blew.

When night descended I was again in my lovely, comfortable, large room with a private bath at the Century Hong Kong Hotel. The building was one of the newer ones on the island containing every modern convenience. A spacious lobby and lounge entrance led to three restaurants; a Chinese Cuisine one, an Italian Cuisine one, and then one of the buffet type serving American and Chinese food. The TV in my attractive room carried a few English speaking channels as well as several in Cantonese.

Around noon the next day Anita and CA arrived at the hotel. They thought the weather was settling enough for a ride up to Victoria Peak.

Of course one important necessity was to eat lunch before any noon time outing. We found a delicious Dim Sum restaurant. This name is another one stemming from a

Province of China and there steamed cooking was the norm. Everything was tasty from the steamed breads to the steamed vegetables and meats. Mango pudding topped off all the other enjoyable dishes.

In order to reach the top of Victoria Peak we sought an air-conditioned bus because heat and humidity are the number one weather forecasts for a good part of the year in this city. Whether the sun is out, or whether it's hazy, or raining, or windy, it's still hot and humid. Almost everything is air conditioned, but there are some buses and stores which aren't. They are sweltering to be in.

Everyone I saw carried a washcloth to wipe the perspiration pouring from their face. The day I arrived Anita handed me a washcloth, and every time we were outside I constantly dabbed at my forehead, upper lip and chin with the cloth. Then each evening my task would be to wash out the cloth and hang it up in order for it to be dry for the next day's use.

Oriental faces are interesting to watch. Until coming to Hong Kong most Chinese people I met seemed to appear very similar in facial construction. But never before was it possible for me to see such a massive group of Chinese in one area. Here the differences were very apparent from eyes to nose to mouth; infant to elderly, short to tall, light skin to dark skin, homely and beautiful all rushing in the streets, standing in queues and packing into transportation. Everywhere we went the same volume of people surrounded us.

The bus ground its way up to the 1200 foot destination and spewed forth a mass of people. Victoria Peak's view of the harbor and the city below proved exceptional. God allowed the clouds and mist to part long enough for us to take a short walk and see the sights below from several different viewing points. Then the spin-off from the Typhoon began and rain came down in a deluge. Fortunately we were carrying our umbrellas with us.

35

We browsed the Mall at the top of the mountain. There were several interesting shops and a 31 Flavors ice cream store. One comical aspect of the merchandise were the T-shirts; all sported Hong Kong scenes, but the labels said they were made in Los Angeles. The opposite is true in Canada or the US with national scenes on shirts being made in the Orient. When I visit a place I want the clothing I buy to be made there.

In most instances the Chinese people here were kind and noble. Usually they showed consideration, but this does not apply to any means of transportation. Push and shove is the name of the game, and it is every man for himself.

We were surrounded by a mass of people waiting for the tram down the mountain. When its door opened everyone acted like they were mad men. Not wanting to be a part of the madness we stood aside until everyone else boarded the vehicle for the steep ride. We were the last on the tram and of course, only standing room was left.

Then something unusual happened - a young man offered me his seat and I was very thankful for his consideration. Especially after seeing the angle the people standing needed to contort into (in order to not fall) while they were hanging on the poles as we traveled down the incline.

Of course it was mealtime again. This night we ate in a restaurant serving European food. I could only eat borsht and French bread as the Dim Sum luncheon still filled me.

The Posts did not have a TV where they were living and I invited them to spend the evening watching the one in my room. Together we enjoyed the change of pace until almost bedtime. Then my friends left for home.

Even though travel time from my hotel room to Anita and CA's condo took about 45 minutes they arrived back at my hotel by eight a.m. the following morning to take me to church. We visited an English speaking Chinese Christian

36

Missionary Alliance Church. The Pastor (a missionary) was home in the states on furlough and this morning's speaker came from the Baptist Denomination. About half of the congregation were Chinese people who either at one time lived abroad, or else they were professional people who used the English language at work.

Several times the Posts mentioned "If you really want to see downtown Hong Kong at its busiest, the time to visit there is Sunday afternoon." The reason for this is because Sunday is the day off for the domestic workers.

They were right! I thought I experienced masses of people in the underground. However nothing could compare to the volume of people on this afternoon. They were in the streets and in the Malls. The bank that looked like an erector battleship contained an open ground floor. There sitting on blankets were family after family of people eating picnic lunches. These people were from the Philippine Islands and are the ones employed in Hong Kong's homes.

One other aspect of this unusual building is when anyone on the open ground floor looks up they can see right into the upper floor because the ceiling is of glass. During the week days the bank's business can be observed from the ground floor.

Everywhere we walked or rode eyes were focused on CA and myself, because we were Ngoi gwok yan (foreigners), or as the less polite phrase goes Gwai lo and Gwai po (white ghost and female white ghost.) If I happened to look at someone who was staring they would shift their eyes. As I looked away they would return to staring at me. I'm sure some of these people were trying to determine if I was a foreigner or Chinese. Several people even asked if I was Chinese. As far as I know my heritage is English, Scottish and French. However, I do have high cheekbones and dark eyes. Even at home I've been asked if I was Chinese or American Indian (especially by students after I teach a course on American Indian Culture).

Dinner reservations for this Sunday evening were for an exclusive shipboard restaurant in Hong Kong Harbor. We were primed for an exceptional dinner in a lovely atmosphere. The Posts' friend George joined Anita, CA and myself for the occasion.

From the dock's view the ship lit up the harbor with its blazing lights and each wave of people preparing to take the launch held their cameras ready for snap shots. We were no different. But with the number of people present it was impossible to achieve a good picture. CA and I decided to wait until after the meal and returned to the dock to take ours.

This floating restaurant's interior was exquisitely decorated in brilliant red and gold. Lovely ladies playing melodious Oriental instruments entertained in the huge dining room. At one end of the room a photographer displayed the ornate traditional Wedding garb in which one client after another encased themselves for pictures.

Anita and CA decided to join the other couples to have their picture taken. Anita looked very authentic, but CA with his height and Caucasian features looked comical. When the high ornate gold hat was placed on his head his appearance became hilarious.

Our reservation was made for eight o'clock, but it was after nine before their picture-taking was over. We received the appetizer of our six course dinner then, and finished eating after ten.

Here I tasted my first Peking Duck and decided then and there it was my favorite Chinese dish. Another new taste for me was shark fin soup. It was very unique and some scientists claim useful in cancer control. The third course was a stir-fried shrimp, vegetable and cashew dish; very tasty. By the fourth course I could eat no more. I'm afraid I failed in the guest etiquette department. Such large meals has not been a part of my diet for quite a few years and my stomach could just not accept any more food.

Despite the lovely surroundings two factors arose which caused uncomfortable feelings this evening. The first being the fact Anita found a spider in her shark-fin soup. After much arguing (in Chinese) the waiter said there would be no charge for the soup. Then when dessert was served a baby cockroach ran across Anita's plate.

At this point CA announced he wanted to see the manager. Much arguing ensued with the waiter, then the maitre'd, but no manager came. By now the time was past ten-thirty at night and only a few customers were still at tables in the room.

Suddenly CA realized the arguing was kept-up to detain us until everyone else left. He stood up and once again said "I want to see the manager" then added "We are leaving now." We walked down the stairs to the launch area while still arguing with the maitre'd. The manager did not appear and still they tried to delay us.

Some of the last customers began to descend the stairs and CA loudly talked about the cockroach. With this the maitre'd said "No charge". He realized others were hearing about the problem. We all boarded the launch and returned to the dock.

With the view of the luminous ship no longer blocked by people we stayed on the dock to take pictures. During this time a group of rough looking men began to gather close to us. Anita heard their Cantonese chatter claiming we were the foreigners who "ripped off" the restaurant by not paying for our meal. Still we ignored them and continued taking pictures. Then we became aware of one the men standing about a foot from CA's back and glaring at him with a menacing stare.

Other restaurant customers standing on the dock saw trouble was brewing and quickly scattered toward a taxi area about a block away. Once we realized the men were ready to fight we joined the rush of departing people and stayed with the group. Three taxies filled before we were able to enter one and get away.

Angels must have surrounded us to prevent the possible injuries which could have taken place. Angry men looking for trouble were prevented from accomplishing the purpose for which they gathered.

Sleep did not come easily this night. All the implications of what could have happened kept popping into my mind. Then too I thought about the clash of cultures. The loss of face for the Chinese maitre'd, versus the Canadian concept of what was accept- able maitre'd etiquette. No wonder there was trouble.

Monday was moving day for me. The next three days and nights I would be staying with CA and Anita in their condominium. They were living in a three hundred square foot apartment which previously belonged to Anita's deceased mother. They were trying to sell the property to settle the estate.

The condo was tiny by North American standards, but average for Hong Kong standards. It contained a bedroom, (large enough for a double bed and chest of drawers) plus an eating-sitting room area. The bathroom and kitchen were both approximately five feet by four and a half feet and there were no cooking facilities except for a one burner hot plate. A small refrigerator sat in the dining area. The bonus point was the fact they were able to also use roof space.

This city of seven million people exhibited row after row of such suites; from government housing to condos used by people of all incomes.

With this being moving day and the business at the University the highlight of Monday came during the evening hours. We held tickets to the Cultural Center's I-Max Theater's presentation of "Life Under the Sea." A very appropriate subject for a city built by the sea.

The setting for the Center itself is on the waterfront with spacious walkways, lovely columns to look at and a huge fountain. This evening the interesting show was presented in English. For three nights each week the film is presented in English. The other nights are in Cantonese.

All the signs in Hong Kong are in duel languages. Directions on public transportation are given in both languages. What surprised me was to find the average person on the street understood little if any of the English language.

Tuesday proved to be very unique and a total immersion day. The Posts took me to Lan Tau Island where an immense Buddha was recently constructed high on a hill top.

Dragon Eyes are a delicious fruit to munch on while taking the picturesque ferry ride to the island. This fruit comes in a gray-tan skin, which peels like a mandarin orange. The edible pulp looks like a huge grape. It was about three-quarters of an inch in diameter and the texture seemed like a grape. Once plopped into my mouth my taste buds enjoyed a new, juicy, mellow flavor. The core of the fruit contained a seed much like one found in a cherry. It didn't take long for the three of us to devour the bag of luscious fruit.

This ferry ride took about an hour. Then we were jiggled on a laboring bus up the side of mountain for another hour. It finally stopped at a huge domicile of temples, gardens and monks quarters. Towering high over us stood the immense Buddha.

We walked into several of the temples, and my heart broke as I saw many people bowing with hands together, making wishes to the stone figures, and placing gifts of food before them; food to be used by the monks residing on the grounds.

41

Outside the air was smoky from a multitude of burning sticks. All the people who previously spent time inside the temple came out to light sticks while hoping the smoke would carry their requests to the god of their Buddha.

There were thousands, upon thousands, upon thousands of people at the site. Beside being in the temples, many of them were ascending and descending the two hundred seventy-five steps to the base of the Buddha, where it sat at the very top of the mountain.

Others were in the huge dining room where meals were being served for one sitting after another. Our meal was scheduled for the one p.m. serving, and after the delicious food we too began the trek up the steps to the island's main attraction. Aged and young clamored up the steps. The infirm crawled on their knees.

Encircling the very base of the figure is a wide platform. We walked around it while enjoying beautiful panoramic sights in all directions. Then we went inside the figure and up two more flights of stairs. The interior held many statues and historic objects.

The late afternoon sun was now low on the horizon. Many people were forming into lines several blocks long. Anita suggested we take a bus in the opposite direction, and then transfer to one traveling to the dock. She thought we would be less crowded.

We waited in line. When the bus came it filled. There were still a dozen people waiting in front of us, as well as all those behind us who were not able to get on the bus. Then we were informed the next bus would not come for another hour.

At this point we thought, "forget it" we'll go get in line to take the bus to the dock. As we walked there CA saw a line at a cab stand which appeared to be shorter. He said he would wait in the cab line and we could go stand in the bus line. Whichever form of transportation came first we would use.

The buses were slow in coming, but finally Anita and I moved forward enough to see we were only about a half block from the bus loading platform. Then CA called for us to join him. The cab line was down to just six people in front of him. We would be eligible for the third cab to come.

As soon as Anita and I left the bus line we saw five busses lumber up the hill. We watched them fill and depart knowing we would have gotten on one if we only stayed in line.

In the meantime cabs came and left, but the people in front of us didn't get into them. Other people out of nowhere pounced on them and entered them.

Again we felt it would be good to separate. Anita and I walked to the end of the now twice as long bus line. Buses came and filled. Taxi's came and filled. Anita and I reached the same position in line as we previously left when again CA motioned for us to join him. He now was holding the door open to a cab.

The taxi flew down the hill to the dock. At any second I expected to be airborne. If there was a race in process, we surely would have won.

Long lines faced us at the dock. One was for the hydrofoil boat, and the other for the regular ferry. With both boats going to the same destination we decided to return to Kowloon on the hydrofoil for a change of pace. The line was also shorter.

CA was happy because he saw people standing in the ferry line, who, at the top of the hill, were waiting in line with him for a taxi. He thought no ground was lost.

We waited about half an hour before the gate was opened to board the hydrofoil. People filed through the gate, then with about ten people in front of us and a long line of people in back of us the gate was closed. We were informed the boat leaving was the last hydrofoil for the day.

One ferry left the same time as the hydrofoil. We looked, and there were no people left in the ferry line, but busses were emptying onto the pier. Like madmen the remainder of the hydrofoil line dashed through and around fences. We were in the lead, and the crush of people was terrible. I prayed the Lord would keep me from fainting, and He did.

Being still in the lead when the ferry gate opened we rushed up the ramp to the portal of open water. I could picture in my mind the mass of people pushing us out the portal, and of our landing in the water. It never happened. When the ferry docked we rushed forward, but the pressure was not as bad as when we went to the ferry entrance.

The ferry's engine sounded like a "clinker" when it started up. It moaned and groaned, rattled and banged with an uneven thump, thump. Halfway across to our destination it stopped. I wondered if we were going to need a tug to haul us into the ferry slip. In a short while a ship passed in front of us and our engine fired up and the realization came, we just stopped to let the boat go bye. My worry was unnecessary.

Because I so enjoyed the Peking duck eaten on Sunday evening the Posts wanted me to have an entire meal of it this evening. We went to a lovely restaurant where the waiter carved the duck at our table. The meat itself is eaten in a wafer thin soft taco-like shell. We put one slice of duck, one sliver of celery and a sliver of green onion, plus a little sauce, then rolled the shell and ate it with our fingers. I enjoyed every bite.

Another specialty of this restaurant was "Poor Man's Chicken". I watched it being served at the table next to ours. First the waiter took a hammer and chisel to break the mud shell the chicken is baked in. Under the shell lotus leaves were peeled back and the very tender chicken was pulled from its bones. The next time I travel to Hong Kong the eating of "Poor Man's Chicken" will be high on my agenda.

Another special activity of this restaurant occurred while we were eating. One of the cooks wheeled out his noodle-making cart and positioned it a few feet from our table. There on top of it sat a huge lump of dough and the cook began stretching it over and over until strands began to separate. Before reaching the final stage for cutting the noodles were stretched until they reached from one extended arm to the other. What a unique demonstration and fun to watch!

My enjoyable visit was drawing to a close with just one more day left before flying home.

After the whirl wind of sightseeing the last day was a quiet one with a short time at the University, plus one final visit to Victoria Peak.

I travel on stand-bye status, and I was informed to report to the Hong Kong airport a little after eleven a.m. There was time to see one more Tai Chi class, and enjoy one more breakfast at the little local Bakery. Good byes were said to the students at the park, and the waiters at the restaurant. Already my heart was sad because of the growing love for these people.

We arrived at the airport on time to find mobs and mobs of people waiting for planes. Because we did not pass where the flags were flown for the notice of approaching Typhoons, we did not know one was coming. Planes were late in arriving, planes were being held, planes were being diverted to other routes.

The ticket agent advised me there would be no use in even getting into line before four-thirty p.m. We went to the University for the afternoon where more good-byes were said.

Hours later, at exactly four-thirty we were back at the airport. There appeared to be no difference in the length of the lines. When I finally reached the ticket agent the woman said, "perhaps you will get on the six-thirty flight, but it will not take off until eight thirty."

I did get on the six-thirty plane, but it was delayed longer than she thought. After taking-on more fuel, because we needed to fly a route different than the usual one, we took off at nine-thirty.

With the plane crossing the international date line we landed in San Francisco at five-thirty p.m. on the same day we took of from Hong Kong at nine-thirty p.m. By now I experienced twenty-six hours of being awake.

My original connection to Seattle took off hours before we landed. Then full planes left every hour to my final destination without room for one more person. I sat in the airport until almost eleven p.m. before there was room for me on a flight. Touch down in Seattle took place at one a.m.; thirty-five hours without sleep for me.

Nine days of exciting wonderful memories are mine. But one poignant memory will always come to the forefront about the many beautiful people in the land of China who have no knowledge of a loving God. Then too, there is some apprehension for the Christians I met. With Communist rule now in force in Hong Kong I wonder if they are suffering persecution? With this possibility how will we ever hear with the silence the government maintains?

IT'S A MIRACLE

Hour upon hour of sitting in an auto repair shop waiting room produces fervent prayer. The saga began 150 miles from home and close to where my daughter lived.

She attempted to start the car. My son-in-law attempted. A grandson attempted. They all said, "I think its your starter." Then they went off to work while I called a towing company.

The car was towed to a starter repair shop. They said, "It's not the starter" and then it was towed to an engine repair place. Upon reaching this point the next five hours were spent sitting in the waiting room with the employees attempting to learn what was causing the problem.

First the verdict was, "It is the timing belt." I explained, "The timing belt was recently replaced." The belt was inspected anyway. Next the opinion came, "It could be the fuses" and they were all tested to find there was no problem. After that I heard, "It could be the computer."

Mounting cost estimates were by now weighing me down and earnest prayers were being sent heavenward. When the shop manager explained there was nothing wrong with the computer, and the only thing left would be the engine itself, I was ready for tears.

Still I could hear the mechanics attempting to turn the motor over. Once more the manager faced me. He said, "Something is very strange because all four valves do not have the right pressure. That never happens! Maybe one or two valves might go, but never all four. I want you to come see so you won't think I'm pulling the wool over your eyes.

Well, I looked and learned where the valves were located. Each was supposed to have a pressure of about 120 degrees. I could see the gauge and read all of them registering below the required amount. This took place while one man manually fed gas, another man manually fed oil, and a third man manually attempted to spark the engine.

The manager said, "Let's try it again." and I leaned over the engine to get a better view. This time all four valves registered the correct pressure. The engine started and the manager yelled, "IT'S A MIRACLE!"

Truly God performed a miracle, but the manager was under the impression I performed it, because my hand touched the car.

Next he wanted me to put my hands on the ears of a deaf mechanic. Then whenever another customer entered the shop he told the miracle story and said the only thing the person's car needed was for me to put my hand on it.

The man's conclusion was embarrassing, funny in a way, but also sad. God did perform a miracle, yet the honor did not go to Him. My declaration, "Only God performs miracles" fell on deaf ears." Oh, that men would praise the living God! Not a mere person.

A PILOT FOR LIFE

Have you ever felt stranded, abandoned, alone, left behind? When a person does much stand-bye flying this is a constant possibility. It has happened to me several times.

One day in the Regina, Saskatchewan airport a full to capacity plane departed and I was not on it. This was the only flight on which it was possible for me to make the connecting plane for the next leg of my journey. There I sat alone in a strange city knowing it would be impossible this day to reach my destination.

Three hours later another full plane was ready to depart for the first leg of my journey. It did not appear I would be able to get on this one either, when the unexpected happened. The gate attendant offered me a ride in the cockpit jump seat (I jumped for it).

For the next hour and a half everything was a new experience for me. How to fit around and into a small seat. How to straddle a cockpit console between my legs while dressed in a skirt. Where to find my oxygen mask and how to exit through the cockpit window in an emergency.

After the preflight check Canadian Regional Airline Captain Brad Murray and First Officer Steve Sanghera graciously explained their actions and moves as they flew. This knob lifts the wheels. Another knob adjusts altitude. One more knob makes the turns. A wheel adjusts the wind resistance. Foot pedals control the rudders and brakes. On and on they offered information. What a gracious crew!

About a half hour before landing the pilot turned on what looked like a TV screen. It sure wasn't a good picture as blips and shadows flitted across the screen. We were flying among storm clouds. Then through the cockpit window I saw a beautiful blue spot and into it we flew while the Captain explained they found the storm-free place on the radar screen and flew into it in order for a bumpy ride to be kept down to the minimum.

The highlight of the whole experience came on the approach to the Calgary, Alberta runway. Right before my eyes we descended for a beautiful landing.

True, my final destination was not reached this day, but I was in a city where people I knew would kindly offer me a night's lodging.

All through this experience the idea kept surfacing, "What a perfect picture of life this short trip has been." Through the rough times, through the good times there is only one safe place to be. It is in life's cockpit with the Lord God Almighty as Captain and seated at His right hand Jesus Christ, the first officer. They know all the correct knobs to move. They know the escape route. They know how to smooth the bumpy places. And they can safely deliver us to our final destination.

A TOUR OF BEAUTY

Foreign destinations with odd sounding names call to many Canadians. We have read of intriguing cities, and looked at pictures of great beauty. Yet to be perfectly honest there is no place more lovely and fascinating than the country of Canada, and specifically the western section. While some people in the Fraser Valley of British Columbia have left home to vacation, others have taken their holiday by showing guests the wonders close to home. One year the latter was the pleasure of this Abbotsford resident.

Guest number one, Annetta, from Philadelphia, Pennsylvania arrived in May. This dear woman became my close friend during our Junior High School years, back in the late 1930's. We lost contact for fifty years until a school reunion took place a few years ago. Then correspondence began across the over 3000 mile expanse; cheery hellos, holiday greetings and finally her acceptance of an invitation to come visit.

With no concept of distance Annetta mentioned in one sentence her long time desire to see Banff, Lake Louise, Jasper and Vancouver. I did not enlighten her about the distance between the places she wanted to visit and planned a circular holiday to fulfill her hearts desire during her two week stay west.

On the morning my friend arrived in the Vancouver airport we went to see some of the city's sights. Have you ever visited Stanley Park? They have a delightful horse and wagon ride, and this became our first adventure. Once on board the driver's descriptive chatter held our attention.

Into the area where the totem poles stand the wagon drew to a halt. Here the driver announced, "Six minute stopover," and everyone left the wagon to get a better view.

A fifty year void in two women's lives causes much chatter. If we weren't talking about "where and when" we were ooh-ing and aah-ing over the flowers and the art work of the totem poles. Then we turned around to find the wagon was not in sight.

There was no problem, we just hailed the next wagon. After explaining what happened all the passengers laughed and the driver told us we would be allowed to climb on if we would sing a song. I started with "Old MacDonald had a farm" and then the wagon began moving with the passengers joining in the singing. Toward the end of the ride the driver pointed out the park restaurant. Annetta and I backtracked to enjoy a tasty belated lunch.

With the repast over we traveled on to the Lions Gate Bridge and up to the Swinging Capilano Bridge. This brave hostess (me) led the two woman tour onto the bucking, heaving, swinging monster, not indicating that she had been too chicken to cross the bridge year after year. Once across we both realized one crossing was enough, but knew the return back to the other side was inevitable. When return time finally arrived some- one dressed in a Smoky the Bear costume waited on our end of the bridge. His purpose was to encourage children across the chasm. Smoky reached out, took Annetta's hand and walked with her across the entire expanse. People chuckled and released some of the fear they were holding when they saw the bear and a grown woman hand in hand.

If you have never taken the challenge of crossing the bridge with your family, perhaps this is the time to think about doing just that. Beside the awesomeness of the chasm there are interesting guides to give pertinent information about the area, also a pictorial history display, interesting shops and across the bridge woodland trails to explore.

A slight haze covered the city, yet the next logical place to visit was Grouse Mountain. As we rode the gondola up the mountain Annetta remarked about all she could see. Once we arrived at the top the huge tourist centre drew us into it to view the area below from all of its platforms and then we went inside to watch a video about the mountain. The last time I was up the mountain was about eight years before and I was now wowed with all of the improvements.

Walking outside of the Centre all of the multi-colored spring wild flowers were bobbing their colorful heads.

After the next day (a Sunday of rest and Worship) the two of us began a seven day trip. For the entire time of travel Annetta's head seemed like it was on a swivel. Off and on I would hear a quiet, "oh, my", or else "why have we never been informed about all of this beauty?"

Our drive began by traveling through the high country of the Coquahalla highway. Then down through the picturesque Okanagan Valley and we ended our first day by browsing through the quaint town of Revelstoke. Day two attempted to rival day one with the panoramic beauty of the Rockies surrounding us.

The car decided the climbing of mountains was not for it. Suddenly the engine was overheating and it became necessary for me to pull to the side of the road. I thought we needed water, but there were no gas stations around to fill the radiator. We limped along and stopped. Then limped along and stopped. Finally we saw a sign for a resort and thinking we would be able to get water there, drove down the lane, away from the highway. After about two miles in we saw the resort, but it was closed.

I stopped the car and waited for the boiling noise to stop, then checked the water. The radiator was full. Next I checked the oil and it was empty. What a predicament! Here we were by a closed resort, in the middle of nowhere, and in order to get to the main highway needed to drive up hill all the way. There was nothing we could do but attempt the drive.

About a quarter of the way up the hill we came to railroad tracks where some men were working. I stopped and told them about our problem and they graciously gave me some of their oil. We were on our way with a car behaving beautifully.

We ate a delicious lunch in the Chalet dining room overlooking frozen Lake Louise, and drove on to peruse the shops and unique stores of Banff. More awesome beauty presented itself the next day with the drive from Banff to Jasper.

Of course the ice fields along the way could not be ignored. The mammoth machine to ride out on the glacier inhaled us and then spit us out onto the ice on a spot way up close to the summit. We were very careful where we walked after the machine driver told us about a man who fell into one of the ice tunnels. He was found the next year floating in the lake at the base of the glacier.

To spend an evening in Jasper seemed very quiet following the business of Banff. We were able to take a breather, yet still shop, before traveling on.

On the Yellowhead Highway our driving took us through more scenic mountains to the city of Prince George, from where we dropped down through ranch country with our goal being a visit to Barkerville.

British Columbia's history comes alive in this authentic gold rush town. There before our eyes were the homes of people who lived in Barkerville a century ago. We saw, and came to understand what life was like for them to travel up the Fraser River and backpack overland to this remote area.

The general store, restaurant, bakery, bar, Chinese laundry, newspaper office, Post Office, doctor and dentist offices, Fire Company, church, and other buildings were open for operation and to view. During summer months the theater presented shows. Even the gold field could be visited. I last visited Barkerville twenty years before. More restoration has taken place since my last being there. The town seemed even more interesting than when I lived not too far from it. To really thoroughly see everything a person should spend a full day in the town.

Only two days were left of our tour. We visited the town of Quesnel, then the remote Baker Creek area west of Quesnel where I once worked. From there Annetta and I traveled south through Williams Lake and the Hells Gate Canyon before finally landing back home in Abbotsford. Truly there in much to see and do in Western Canada.

The close to Annetta's and my fun time together loomed before us. There seemed much more we could do, but it was now necessary to pick and choose what most appealed for the final days of sight seeing.

Mt. Baker, which can be seen from my windows, drew us for one day. However when we reached the parking lot high on the mountain everything was snow covered. The pictur-esque trails were unapproachable. After driving the 60 miles to get there, the only thing we could tell anyone anything about seemed to be the time we spent traveling on the road, but we could say, "We went up Mt. Baker."

Still there were places close to Abbotsford where we planed take a day trip. Bridal Falls certainly was one of them. Annetta and I leisurely strolled the fifteen minute walk to the base of one of the most inspiring views up the face of a cliff where the lacy appearing water descended.

Harrison Lake could not be left out. Such a beautiful expansive sight greets the eyes of anyone walking the path along the beach. Of course we also needed to go inside the pool area and actually see where people bathed in the Hot Spring water.

And the perfect ending for a two week holiday is a stroll around Queen Elizabeth Park in Vancouver. We were there between the blooming seasons. The rhododendrons were finished and the roses were not yet in bloom. Yet the paths were pleasant to walk, the view of the city was spectacular, and the statues eye catching. Neither of us were disappointed because we went there.

From the park we were off to Steveston to enjoy lunch in one of the waterfront restaurants. The shops are attractive in this little historic town and it was necessary for us to browse each of them. A delight to us was to find a recently opened fish canning museum. Then the delight was squelched because the visiting hours were over for the day (another day, another guest and I will visit Steveston during the hours the museum will be open). Lastly we walked through the riverside park. That is, we walked as far as the first bench and sat. After two weeks of constantly being on the go it felt good just to sit and watch others (people and boats) go bye. Our pleasant memories will remain for a long time.

Guests number two arrived in the month of June to celebrate the birthday of my granddaughter. Ann wanted a visit to Victoria for her birthday gift. She, her two sisters, Tanya and Krystal, her cousin Laura, her niece Hannah, plus her Aunt Pauline (my daughter) never before went to visit to our Province's capital. The desire for this particular gift was brought about by the chatter of Ann's mother, Patti, from a visit she made there. Naturally Patti joined our group so she could go again.

Five of the group arrived at my home on Friday evening. The sixth on Saturday morning. To make the occasion truly unique we planned to travel by bus.

The morning bus left Abbotsford at 9:30 a.m., and arrived in Victoria at 3:30 p.m. This included a bus change in Vancouver, plus the ferry ride across the Straight of Georgia.

All went well until we arrived in Victoria. The motel clerk told us on the phone there would be a fifteen minute walk from the bus terminal to the motel. We opted to walk. However six adults, with two children, one under one year of age, plus six suitcases, a play pen, a car seat and a stroller could not cover the distance in less than thirty minutes.

Tea at the Empress Hotel was scheduled for five o'clock. The crazy trip became worth every minute of travel to taste the luscious sandwiches and desserts; to sit in the lovely hotel dining room and later to view the beauty of the harbor as we strolled the attractive walkway.

From the water front the eight of us took the bus to Buchart Gardens. Feasts for the eyes followed one after another for the next three hours. In daylight and under night light each garden area exhibited its own beauty.

Eleven thirty at night all of us dragged our fatigued bodies into the comfortable lodging accommodations. As far as we were concerned the reason for the trip now drew to an end. On the next morning a bus would be boarded for the return trip to Abbotsford.

Actually the time spent at our destination seemed so very short. It definitely whetted the appetites of my family members to visit Victoria again for a longer stay. But never to make the trip by bus again.

Guests number three, CA & Anita Post, from Wisconsin, arrived in July. Their stay was for only two days and I took them to some of the familiar sights which Annettta saw in Vancouver and the Fraser Valley. Still there were more sites to visit. One was the unique hilltop location of Westminster Abbey, in Mission, from where a magnificent panoramic view of the River valley could be observed. Of course the

57

modern architecture of the Abbey's Worship centre also was inspected.

Another feature we went to see is located in Seven Oaks Mall. It is the one-of-a-kind water clock. We arrived there at ten minutes to the hour in order to watch the whole procedure of the water emptying from minute to minute, then into the hour. With the scientific minds of both CA & Anita they were fascinated. On leaving the Mall we drove around the corner for a view of placid, shimmering Mill Lake with the moon rising over Mt. Baker as a back drop. The Posts left with Lovely! Lovely! Lovely! on their lips.

One more trip, a day one, was made with a friend, Betty Kirsch who lives in the town of Mission (located across the Fraser river from Abbotsford). This became an August holiday to Minter Gardens. We were enthralled with the many flower arrangements of exquisite blooms and enchanted with the floral figurines and various types of gardens. With the temperature not too hot, nor too cool, the hours of walking trails turned into pure pleasure.

Now the summer is practically over. Time will pass before guests visit again. Still when they come there will be places to go which they have not seen before; Cultus Lake, Fort Langley, Wonderland, Aldergrove Zoo, and more. We live in one of the most beautiful and unusual places in the world. Everyone who visits me remarks about their being awed by God's handy-work all around us.

YOU NEED TO GO

Why did I need to go? The reason wasn't apparent to me and there just seemed many reasons not to go. First, because some research needed to be completed for a manuscript I was working on. Secondly, because a possible imminent death of a family member might take place while I was gone. Then too, the travel itself would consume time, which could be used otherwise. Lastly some things around my home really should be taken care of.

Yearly, a Mission Conference was a part of my agenda. But, this year one reason after another flooded my mind to make my attendance there seem impractical. Still the thought about trying to go kept nagging me.

The actual travel time turned out to be quite an ordeal. Through part of it I would question, "Lord, do you want me to go?" The following thought kept surfacing, "Yes, you need to go!"

Because I am able to fly standby on a certain airline, and because more flights are available from the city where my two daughters live, I usually drive the three hours to one of their homes and they take me to the airport. This saves on the cost of leaving my car at the airport parking lot, or the cost of taking an airport shuttle from home. Both are more expensive than the gas used for the drive.

Airport arrival time for me was five a.m. On the following morning at five a.m. I was still sitting in the same airport. Seven planes to my destination filled and departed during the twenty four hour wait. Being the month of August all planes were overbooked. After the early morning flight on the second day left the gate personnel told me, "All of today's flights are overbooked."

Suddenly the time was right to shift to plan B. Step one required taking a bus to my daughter's home. Step two was to pick up my car and drive the 150 miles home. Step three became to pay the full price of a ticket on a different airline. Step four included a car rental at the destination airport.

Beside all of the steps necessary to finally arrive in Calgary, Alberta, there followed an uncomfortable experience with customs. The question was, "Why did your suitcases come on one airline while you arrived on a different one?" Of course my suitcases were checked when I attempted to fly standby. I arrived twenty-four hours later. Every article in each suitcase was put through much scrutiny by customs. Once the long story was explained, and confirmed by the airline agent, my bags were released and I journeyed on.

With the night before being sleepless I wasn't too "with it" while driving a rental car to the Conference. The hour was late afternoon and I knew my arriving at the camp- ground would be too late to eat dinner, so I stopped at a fast food place. After finishing my hamburger and walking outside the realization came - the car is no where to be seen. Immediately my thoughts were "my car has been stolen", and I made an extra good search through the parking lot in case the car was in a different parking spot than what I thought it should be. My white Honda was not anywhere. The only sensible thing to do was to go call the police. Then it dawned on me - I wasn't driving my Honda, but a blue rental car. The blue car was right where I parked it and I really felt dumb.

My arrival to the Conference ground was almost bed time. As soon as my head hit the pillow I fell sound asleep because of just spending forty-three hours of being awake. The following day's messages were inspirational and the fellowship proved to be exceptional.

In my business during the previous months I never realized my need to get away from every- day work to listen to a special speaker dig into the Word of God. Nor did I know of my hunger for the fellowship of other people involved in the same ministry I was involved with. Each of us who were at the Conference still serve within the same organization, but the majority of us no longer live close enough to each other to share our lives.

Truly, I needed to attend the Conference. It was like a silent hunger stalked me until I became starved and now finally was fed. The blessing of being there continued to linger for weeks.

IT'S SUPPOSED TO BE A HOLIDAY

Flight number 874 turned out to be an hour late leaving the Dallas airport for New York City. It was also an hour late arriving at its destination. This shrunk the possible commute time within the city from the LaGuardia airport to the JFK airport from three hours to two hours. It should have been plenty of time to make my connecting flight for overseas.

Rain was falling and traffic was heavy, but the main concern of the shuttle passengers was the fact being this day was the driver's first day on the route. Once we arrived on the JFK property the driver turned the van onto a surface road. We became stuck behind one stopped vehicle after another. Time ticked away! Blood pressure rose! A van full of upset people fumed! Few of us made our connecting flights.

Here I was a woman alone in New York City. First I thought I would just stay in the airport, but the airline agent advised against it. She arranged for me to stay in the motel where the stewardesses stay. They were to send a courtesy car, bit it never came to where I waited.

A half hour later the agent called the motel receptionist again to tell her of my plight. Now they said to take a cab and the fare would be deducted from the bill. The motel was supposed to be a ten minute drive from the airport.

Problem number four came when the motel's location was not a familiar one to the cab driver and he needed to ask his supervisor the directions. Once on the road the two of us saw the motel's sign from the freeway as we passed the street where it was located. Three times the cab driver missed the exit and three times he circled through neighborhood streets trying to locate it before getting back on the freeway. When we pulled into the motel entrance the cab meter read $35.

One of the highlights of my trip came next (it was downhill most of the rest of the evening). Here the Lord's arrangement was for me to be in the back seat of a moral, honest cab driver.

The man turned around and said to me "I will only charge you the regular fare of $7, because the mistake was mine."

Into the motel I walked to find the entire receptionists area surrounded with bulletproof glass. How discouraging for anyone entering. At waist level there was a small hole to pass a credit card or cash into the receptionist.

With registration taken care of I headed toward my ground floor room, and while walking down the hall a door opened slightly in front of me. There stood a man who invited me into his room and I assured him I was not interested. The hair on the back of my neck stood up when the realization came that my door was across from his. There were three locks on the door and once inside all were firmly locked.

Being safely inside didn't help when I soon knew it would be needful to leave the security of my room. The time was now eight p.m. and I was hungry. My stomach's only nourishment from early in the morning was a cup of yogurt and a muffin at noon.

When first walking into the lobby I noticed a restaurant on one side. This was the destination toward which my feet carried me. Dangling in the window a sign stated, "Closed on Sundays." This was Sunday. Walking outside the motel's door would not seem sensible to do and I asked the receptionist about ordering food. He put me through to a Chinese restaurant.

Forty-five minutes later a delivery man arrived at my door. The Chinese man spoke very broken English and it seemed his only concern was as to whether I was Chinese or not. After finding out I wasn't, he wanted to know what nationality I was. With that settled the food was finally handed me. It was not good Chinese food, but half was consumed because of hunger.

Now the time was past nine o'clock and I turned on the TV to see a picture which was completely foreign to me. It took me several seconds before the realization came about the channel being a pornographic one. Off the TV went. The only thing left for me to do to relax would be to read, and I dug a book out of the suitcase.

The book marker fell out and its inscription "Behold, I am with you and will keep you where ever you go." Gen. 28:15 leaped out at me. Utter peace descended and later sleep came for the short time until the early morning flight.

How gracious God was to remind me of His protection. Also assuring is the fact God continually teaches me about how He goes through the problems of life with me.

HAIR STOOD UP IN FRIGHT

The airport shuttle was a half-hour late in picking me up. A pleasant driver did not seem at all perturbed over his lateness and graciously opened the van door for me.

Then time was taken to stop for two more passengers, and we were off to the airport. The friendly passengers greeted me. A round of questions followed; where each was from, where each was going? Then questions about their profession, etc.

Once the other two people found I lived in Canada, was a teacher, a missionary, and worked with North American Indian people questions came in abundance. I ended up sharing my life history and the need for people in every culture to have a personal relationship with Jesus Christ.

The churchgoing man in the front seat and the agnostic lady sitting next to me both understood how to accept Christ as their Saviour by the time we pulled into the airport.

Both people departed the van for the same airline and the driver drove on to my stop. During this period of time the driver, in very broken English, said to me, "You know, I always carry my gun on my dashboard."

Hair stood up on the back of my neck and I thought, "O God, what have I gotten myself into now?"

The man stopped the van, picked-up the object on the dashboard and walked around to let me out of the vehicle.

As I stepped down he showed me his gun. It was a Bible, the driver's modern day weapon. Praise the Lord, this man was an unknown prayer warrior who was praying as I answered the questions on the way to the airport.

WHAT CAN HAPPEN NEXT?

A beautiful fall day dawned with sunshine, making the drive from lower B.C. to Anacortes, Washington lovely (not a dependable factor with the area's fame for cloudy, inclement weather.) My objective for this day was to spend an afternoon with a prayer partner out on Orcas Island. The time of ferry departure was 1:10 p.m., which would put me on the island at 2 p.m.

I left home at nine in the morning to allow myself time for a bite to eat in the ferry terminal before boarding the boat. The old adage about the "best laid plans of mice and men", or else "Murphy's law", came into play at this point. Upon reaching the terminal my ears heard, "The one o'clock ferry broke down. We won't have another one here until two o'clock." Plus, "The food concession in the terminal is closed."

Plan number two now came into effect, which was to find a place to eat and a phone to notify the people on the island I would be a hour late. With the two objectives accomplished the beautiful ferry ride through the San Juan Islands became a feast for the eyes.

My prayer partner met me on the Orcas Island dock and before we drove off he asked the ferry agent about the return schedule. Bill was assured every ferry would be at least one hour late.

In the home meeting we chatted and then I showed the mission's video to Bill and the other family members. For dinner my prayer partner took me to a picturesque restaurant on the waterfront located close to the ferry dock. The quaint, homey atmosphere exhibited a colonial decor with each table even having its own hurricane coal oil lamp. Every plate of food looked like an artist was at work and the taste was delicious.

Horror, of horrors - just as the main course was served we saw out the window the ferry coming into dock. I hastily cut my meat, as the waiter rushed for a container. The lovely looking food was dumped into a plastic container while Bill and I prepared to make a mad rush to the dock.

My fine food was eventually eaten with a plastic fork while perched on a stool in the ferry's quick-food eating area. However, the flavor was not affected at all. As a matter of fact I relished each tasty morsel.

All went well from this point until I was about forty-five minutes from home.

On a dark, narrow, windy road I heard a siren approaching and in the rear view mirror flashing lights appeared. After pulling to the side of the road two police cars rushed past me.

About one-half mile from the Canadian border the night sky seemed lit with a tremendous amount of flashing lights. The road was completely blocked and an officer came to me to ask where I was going. I replied, "Through the border crossing." His retort was, "You will have to find another one."

Not until the next evening's news did I understand what I was involved in. The newscaster told of a Canadian man commandeering a bus and crashing through the border into the U.S. When I arrived on the scene the stopped bus was surrounded with gun-wielding police and the man was choking a passenger. He was then captured and charged with illegally crossing the border with a bus containing kidnapped passengers.

No matter what kind of situation I find myself in, I am thankful for the peace

God can give through the experience.

WORDS YOU DON'T WANT TO HEAR

Smoothly the plane flew from Seattle toward St. Louis, Missouri. There was no turbulence in the lovely blue sky and with the plane being moderately full I enjoyed three seats all to myself.

On our final approach into the airport the pilot's voice came over the loudspeaker saying, "We are five minutes from touchdown and must abort the landing. There is a brake problem and we will try to take care of it from here."

A male passenger sarcastically said in a loud voice, "What are they going to do crawl out on the wing?"

I began to mightily pray, "Oh Lord, protect this plane. Put your mighty hands under these wings and deliver us safely to the ground."

Fifteen minutes later the pilot's voice could be heard once more. He said, "Our landing wheels are now down and we will land. Then taxi a long way before stopping."

The first thought in my mind was - the landing wheels were not down before. What a terrible plight we were in without the braking power of wing flaps down and no landing wheels.

We touched down at a greater speed than usual. Mid screeching, grinding noises coming from the wheel brakes we traveled down the runway. Then past one building after another; on and on; finally stopping at the far end of another runway. An audible sound could be heard throughout the plane as people exhaled.

God's protection is perfect. He even told us so in the Bible, "Behold, I am with you and will keep you wherever you go."

While many people automatically expect their creator to keep them safe there are times when the Lord allows us to go through terrifying experiences. Our Saviour wants us to realize how magnificent is His Father's protecting power through our specifically asking for His help and then see it take place. Then we need to thank the Almighty for answering our prayer.

EAGLES AND DOLPHINS AND WHALES

Alaska - the last frontier - the land of the midnight sun! And what else? Only a trip there will reveal the secret.

Sometimes traveling brings unsuspected experiences. This trip began with one, and from then on they never stopped popping up.

Annetta, my friend from Philadelphia, Pennsylvania flew into the Vancouver, British Columbia airport. Her luggage must have gone to Timbuktu, as it was not with her. At nine-thirty on a Monday evening we debated about how to solve the problem of obtaining her luggage. We needed it immediately because we were to leave the next morning to drive a 1000 miles north to the Alaska ferry terminal, only one solution could be reached. This was to have the bags delivered to the northern Prince Rupert ferry terminal.

In the meantime Annetta packed a few of my slacks and tops into her overnight bag; for her to use until her suitcase was recovered.

Once on the road spectacular views greeted our eyes in every direction while winding north through the Coastal Mountains up to Whistler's ski resort and on and on. The mountains, glaciers, waterfalls and bubbling streams were awesome. Our accommodations ranged from rustic, to quaint, to comfortable, and the food everywhere seemed superb.

Confidently we walked into the Prince Rupert terminal to claim our luggage and the words we heard were, "Oh, a suitcase arrived a couple of days ago, but we weren't authorized to accept it, so we refused the bag. Perhaps it is still at the airport.

A frenzied phone call made it possible for us to obtain the bag before the ferry left. However this was just the beginning of our not knowing what would be happening next. When I gave our tickets to the agent she said, "The ferry schedule is completely changed. Your first destination is as scheduled, but all of the rest will be a day later in sailing." This meant half of the prearranged motel reservations would need to be canceled or changed. It would not be an easy job with the huge influx of summer visitors to Alaska. Most accommodations would be full.

Laying aside the thought of the future accommodations problem Annetta and I set about enjoying the comfort of the Alaska ferry system. Situated at the front of one of the decks was a lounge with a wraparound window to view the beautiful scenery to the right, the left, as well as what was in front of the vessel. There we situated ourselves in either a straight-backed chair or a recliner. At meal time the dining room served tasty meals, and our cabin sleeping quarters were clean and comfortable.

This sailing adventure begins with the six p.m. departure from Prince Rupert, and our arrival on the island of Petersburg followed the next day at noon. With plan A our departure from St. Petersburg would be twenty-four hours later. However it was necessary to shift to plan B because one of the Alaska fleet's ferries experienced a fire and was out of service. Of course the ferry fire was on the boat we were originally to depart from Petersburg. With plan B our layover was 48 hours instead of 24.

When Annetta and I checked into the Sandia Motel in St. Petersburg I told the receptionist about our problem and the need to stay a second night. She responded, "We are full, but I will put your name on a waiting list in case there is a cancellation."

Before the two of us went sightseeing I phoned our future motels to advise them of the situation. In both Sitka and Juneau the reservations were for two nights. There was no problem in canceling the first night and keeping the second night. But when I tried to reserve a room for another night I received the same response as was given in Petersburg, "We are full."

Picturesque Petersburg was founded by people of Scandinavian heritage. Their culture could be felt in the shops and in the way of life of this fishing village. Annetta and I browsed our way along the small shopping area in the center of town. Then we visited the tourist bureau.

From the brochures two interesting areas caught our attention for places to see. One was the museum, and the other a nature reserve located a few miles from town at the end of the paved road. One question I asked the tourist bureau agent was, "What time is tomorrow's Sunday service at the Presbyterian Church.

Before dinner we visited the museum and then enjoyed a good meal at a lovely waterfront restaurant. I spent an hour or more in the evening calling the Bed and Break- fast accommodations on the island to find they also were all full.

Then when walking through the lobby the next morning on my way to attend church the motel receptionist called me over to tell me, "I'm sorry, but we have received no cancellations and I called the other motel in town. They too are full." I pictured in my mind Annetta and I spending the night in the car.

The church's parking lot looked deserted when I arrived fifteen minutes before the service time given to me, but the door was open, so I walked in. Inside a lady greeted me and told me the service took place two hours earlier (the tourist bureau was not aware of the summer time hour). The remaining people who were there stayed for a planning meeting about how to reach out into the community. They invited me to stay, and when they learned I was a missionary they were convinced I was sent from God to be at their meeting to give them information on outreach.

As a child I remember my Presbyterian pastor talking about missions in Alaska. As a teenager I remember praying for a specific missionary serving in Alaska. Now as a Senior citizen an unexpected door was opened for me to share in a church planted by the missionaries heard about forty years earlier.

At the end of the meeting I shared the circumstances Annetta and I found ourselves in. Immediately a home was offered in which we could stay. We were to arrive there in time for dinner.

Following some lunch Annetta and I drove out to the nature reserve to enjoy a pleasant stroll. We found a boardwalk on top of soft spongy ground with sparse plant life and over it we meandered down to a picturesque river. Many animal foot impressions could be seen in the soft soil. Some of them were bear prints.

Several fishermen stood casting their lines into the water, and immediately a fish would bite. Annetta and I watched the fish splash and fight, but inevitably the fisher- man won. We could see there would be fish for dinner on his table this night, and some for the freezer once the large salmon was brought to the river bank.

The lovely shore front home of Brian and Marjorie Paust was the Lord's provision for our sleeping place. Their pic- ture windows viewed the water, across which sat beautiful mountains with glaciers

It seemed like Marjorie, along with her daughter Becky (home from college), were gourmet cooks. Fried chicken, along with king crab, baked potatoes and a delicious salad sprinkled with colorful pansies tantalized the taste buds of the three Pausts, one of Becky's friends, Pastor Ralph Mueller, Annetta and myself. We enjoyed delicious food and sweet fellowship.

During breakfast the next morning we watched six deer strolling along the water's edge. The blessings of God's creation awed us.

Soon our stay in Petersburg drew to a close and the time there will remain memorable. Annetta, who is of Jewish ancestry and does not claim Jesus as her Messiah, remarked several times, "The Pausts opened their home to us when they didn't know us." Or else she said, "They were of German descent and seemed so friendly." Annetta lost many family members during the Nazi extermination of the Jewish people. Here she saw a side of German people she was not aware of, and God used a unique situation to express and impress Christian love to a woman of His chosen race whom He loves.

We left Petersburg at three p.m. for a lovely ferry ride to Sitka. Along the way we were treated to the sight of several whales leaping, diving and blowing. At dusk a heavy mist covered the whole area while the ship slid through narrow passageways. There were several spots where a lookout was placed at the front of the boat to make sure there was no danger before us. Sitka's arrival was two a.m. the next morning and we were very ready for sleep. The motel room would be ours until eleven a.m.

This Alaskan island also held much history and was very unique in the culture brought by the early Russian settlers. The flavor from the old country was apparent in the architecture, plus in the wares for sale in the shops. Alaska's oldest Russian Orthodox church is located in Sitka. We visited in the church, and then we went out to a museum located on the campus of the Shedon Jackson Christian

College, where we saw the largest collection (in the world) of Alaskan Native art.. We examined display after display, shelf after shelf, isle after isle of artifacts and gained more insight into the Native way of life.

Before leaving the motel the receptionist mentioned she thought the college rented dorm rooms to tourists. Naturally, when we were on campus we stopped in the office to inquire about rooms. Our needs for a night's accommodations were once again supplied because of a Presbyterian Christian influence on an Alaskan island. We enjoyed an exceptionally good dinner for a college dining doom and slept in a comfortable bed for the night.

Ferry departure from Sitka was five a.m. and we were on board with bleary eyes. However, our eyes were soon opened to all the ethereal beauty along the shore line of mountains and glaciers all draped in wispy clouds and mist. Then too every once in a while everyone on board would become aware of dolphins in the water, seals perched on buoys, or eagles soaring; sometimes even whales cavorting.

Darkness was all around when the ferry pulled into the Juneau dock and we sought a Motel 8 where our reservations were previously made for this night. Sleep was sweet and sightseeing was scheduled for the next day. However, before leaving the motel room in the morning our objective was to locate another night's housing.

Annetta mentioned that before coming on the trip she was given a brochure about the Alaska Hotel in downtown Juneau. Many years ago the building was built for the gold rush crowd. Today, although there are rooms still available to rent it is considered a Historical landmark with all of the old flavor.

Rooms for our use were open. Rooms which fit right into the gold rush decor and age; small in size with antique furniture. We did have a private bath in what was once a closet. The rooms were located on the third floor and there was no elevator. However beds for the night were something to be thankful for.

Now we could explore the interesting town and shops. Juneau is built on the side of a mountain with a tram to travel to the very top. From there our view of the town, the water and the mountains was breathtaking.

Another inspiring sight in this Alaskan capital is the Mendenhall glacier; our early afternoon destination. We looked at the glacier from several different directions. One was from the viewing platform inside the building on the site. This tourist area also offered an interesting movie on the development of the glacier (we also saw a similar type movie on the mountain top). Close to the glacier we watched many spawning salmon swimming in a mountain stream.

As the dinner hour approached Annetta and I were riding in the town's sight- seeing trolley down the street where our hotel was located. The conductor pointed up and said, "See those third floor windows?" That is where the ladies of the night display their wares." The two of us gulped and chuckled. Our rooms were the third floor ones. In this day we experienced traveling from the sublime to the ridiculous.

The last leg of our ferry ride went from Juneau to Haines. One more early ferry to catch, but the ride was only until noon when we arrived at the quaint seaside town. This day's goal was to sightsee during the afternoon. Then drive the next morning toward the Alcan highway.

Annetta and my time on the water and in Alaskan coastal towns was different than what we expected, but very enjoyable. There were salmon and halibut meals, plus the excitement of unexpected lodging and beautiful scenery all around in every direction. God blessed us over and over the entire week.

One tourist attraction most people who visit Alaska want to see is Glacier Bay. The ferry system does not sail into the Glacier area and Annetta did not want to go home to tell people she wasn't able to see the glacier. We knew there were local flights over the bay from the town, so we walked into a travel agent office to see if Annetta could book a flight. I was not interested in going because I visited there a few years before and did not now want to pay the cost of the flight for something already seen.

While we were in the Travel Bureau a little Korean woman with a Caucasian man entered and Annetta asked, "Where are you going?" The man responded, "To hell!" We were rather shocked with his response and said no more.

Later in the afternoon Annetta and I were standing on a corner discussing where we wanted to next visit, when the little Korean lady came up to us. We could tell by the expression on her face she was very upset and the story she told in broken English sent chills up our back.

The woman was a teacher from Korea who came to Canada to visit. While south she met the man we saw her with, and he promised to take her sightseeing all the way to Alaska. When she agreed to travel with him he took all of her possessions, including her money, and told her he would take care of her. She did not know how she was going to get back down to Vancouver in order to fly home.

Because we were standing on the corner where a bank was located I took the woman in to talk to one of the agents. We learned the woman still held her visa card, therefore she could purchase a plane ticket. However to fly from Haines to Vancouver she must go by way of Seattle. Then the little lady showed us her ticket from Vancouver to fly back to Korea. We were sure then that what she was telling us was not scam.

I wanted to take her to the local Pastor in order for her to be safe for the night. He would make sure she would get her ticket for the plane back to Vancouver. She was excited and wanted to go back to the man to tell him she just learned how she could get back to Vancouver. I could not dissuade her and we parted company. For days afterward I wondered what happened to her.

Because the weather turned unstable Annetta's flight over Glacier Bay was canceled. We left the next morning to drive east to the Alcan highway.

The highway is an experience unto itself. Not much can rival the breath- taking views from the Alaska border down through the Yukon to mile zero in Dawson Creek, British Columbia.

All along the road can be seen rugged mountains, glaciers, dense forests, and a multiple supply of wild life; caribou, bears, coyote, wolves, plus majestic eagles soaring overhead.

No one can say the road is like a freeway, nor can you safely travel over 50 miles an hour and have your car remain in one piece. Some people claim the road is paved. The truth is there are paved patches, much gravel, and spots where it is a challenge to drive through soft dirt and deep gullies. At these places there are usually working road crews who stop what they are doing to watch if you make it through. They always have a surprised look on their faces when a woman successfully manages to not get stuck.

We found drivers who had no knowledge about driving on gravel. They thought they were on a freeway, and attempted to drive at freeway speed. One such person pulling a travel trailer passed me. I ended up completely engulfed in dust and could not see a thing, but did hear a ping, ping, ping, five times. It was gravel leaving cracks on my windshield.

Space between settlements, gasoline stations, and res- taurants makes reaching any destination hours away. With this in mind before we drove away from Haines, Annetta and I purchased a sack lunch to take along.

A little after the noon hour we were traveling along a lovely lake. There we stopped to eat and found even dry bread tasted good with hunger and a lovely scene in view.

The road etiquette along the Alcan is to stop and help when a car is parked by the side of the road with people sitting in it. A kind man stopped while we were eating lunch and then went on when he found we were not in trouble.

One other item to note - there are no porta-potties in the wilds along this road. However , the grass is tall and there are lots of woods.

During our four day drive south there were some noteworthy stopping places. They were usually attained at the end of a long day's drive.

Annetta and I arrived in the town of White Horse, Yukon on the weekend the city was holding their annual Rodeo; visitors were everywhere. We planned to attend the main event on Sunday afternoon for the eastern city girl Annetta to see a sport she never viewed before.

First on any Sunday morning it was important to me to take time to worship the Lord. I looked in the phone book on Saturday night to make sure of the service's time Two hours were listed; one for summer and one for winter. Fifteen minutes before the appointed summer hour I arrived at the Whitehorse Baptist church to find everyone seated and the Pastor was almost through his sermon.

A short time later on leaving the church I handed the Pastor my card and asked him what time the service began. It was the time listed in the phone book. What I didn't know was there was a time change between Alaska and the Yukon.

The Pastor looked at my card and said, "June Temple, I know you." I was surprised and asked him, "How do you know me?" Then I learned the man was a fill-in for the Pastor who was on vacation. He was a missionary with a sister organization ministering to Canadian tribal people, and a few summers before attended a combined Conference for Native workers which I also attended.

Now for the Sunday afternoon Rodeo finals. The two of us enjoyed watching the barrel-racing, calf-roping, plus bronco and bull-riding. But our day didn't end with this event.

After dinner we took a boat ride up the Yukon River through the rapids. It took about an hour and a half going up against the swirling current, but because of the swift- ness of the water, on the return trip we were back to the dock in 45 minutes. With a full day under our belts we were ready for a good night's sleep.

Early the next morning Annetta and I were traveling to Watson Lake where the zero mark of the Alcan highway is located and it was supper time when we arrived there. A motel was found, then the first thing on our agenda was a stop at "The Wall".

During the Second World War lonely GI's who were building the Alcan highway hung their home state auto plates on a wall. The tradition has continued with today's tourists adding theirs. There are now several walls full of licensee plates from all over Canada, the United States and other parts of the world.

Two more days of driving stretched ahead of us. We did stop for about a half hour at the hot springs south of Watson Lake and then stayed that night in Dawson Creek. On we went to spend the last night in the town of Quesnel.

Much of what is read and heard about Alaska is true. It is a land of uniqueness. It is the last frontier, it has its own peculiar beauty, it is barren, and it is miles away from the lower forty- eight. However, nothing can compare to the enjoyment of visiting there with a good friend.

ISRAEL and EGYPT

For 55 years, ever since I became a Christian, the place in this world I most desired to visit was the land where my Saviour walked while He lived on earth. Finally the opportunity and the funds became available.

The Pastor of Calvin Presbyterian church (where I often attended in my home town) announced from the pulpit, "My wife and I will be leading a tour to Israel in the spring." When Hans Kauwenburg made this announcement my heart desired to go on the trip. But right at the moment my purse did not have the funds to do such a thing, so I started to pray about the matter, and God provided.

Early in the month of March there were 15 people from Calvin church, and five other people (who heard of the tour and wanted to join us) meeting at the airport for our morning flight to Tel Aviv. Late the next afternoon we landed at our destination and settled into a lovely hotel located on the Mediterranean Sea.

Even though the flight was a long one none of us wanted to spend the evening in a hotel room. We soon were walking the lovely paved path along the sea while the sun descended and the moon rose. I contemplated taking a swim, but was advised there were sharks. It was just as well. By nine p.m. the long flight was finally catching up with me.

The next morning we met our guide who was a very knowledgeable Arab Christian named Peter. His family had resided in Jerusalem for 700 years.

We boarded our bus for the first leg of the journey going south to the town of Joppa. While we were traveling there Peter reminded us about the apostle Peter being in Joppa when the vision of the blanket full of unclean animals was lowered before him and he was told to eat.

Across from the place pointed out to us as being where this incident happened was the church of St. Peter. Our guide joked about many of the churches in Israel being named after him.

Then our guide reminded us of Joppa being the village from where Jonah departed for his sea voyage to Tarshish. A sudden awe came over me when I realized I was viewing Old Testament historical places, not just the places at the time of Christ, but places in history way before Christ was ever born.

The bus only made a short jog through the village and then we traveled the road north up to Caesarea; everyone enjoyed the coastal scene to our left.

Caesarea's desolation grabs a person. Once King Herod lived there and he saw to building of engineering marvels during his time. No one lives there now, but the place is being restored in order for tourists to view what the city once was.

The first building we saw under restoration was a monstrous sized open theater. Everyone sat on the stone bleachers in the theater and looked out over the beautiful sea. Our guide told us the harbor we were looking at was one of the area's marvels built by Herod's engineers.

There was no harbor when Herod first arrived in Caesarea. He ordered the entire waterfront to be dredged and lined with rocks (hauled from the hills) in order for large ships to be able to drop anchor. This is where the Cedars of Lebanon arrived to be used in Biblical construction projects.

We roamed around an old Roman Fort, a Crusader Chapel and looked at some of the restoration work before boarding the bus again. Our next stop was only a few miles from Caesarea at an ancient viaduct in very good condition. One more marvel built by Herod lay before our eyes. The viaduct looked in very good shape for having stood 2000 years without any work being done on it. At the time when Herod lived in Caesarea there was no fresh water in the seaport and the viaduct was constructed to bring spring water several miles from the hill country to the city.

Now north we traveled up to the Mountain where Elisha called down fire from heaven and all of us stood a short while overlooking the lovely Valley of Armageddon far below us. Then the bus moved on until we reached the town of Nazareth.

How surprising to learn many of the people of Nazareth lived in the caves of the town during the time of Christ. We looked into one and our guide said, "In all probability Mary and Joseph lived in one like this."

Our group visited a lovely church in the center of the old city over the place where it is believed the angel appeared to Mary. Another fact told us was - "a church has been standing on this site since the second century."

Before we left Canada each of us were given a small supply of pins with the Canadian flag on them. We made quite a "hit" with the children of Nazareth as we walked by them and handed out the pins.

Next to old Nazareth sat new Nazareth. Our guide mentioned the fact about many of Israel's towns were now designated into old and new sections. The new being where people live who have moved to the country since the second world war and, of course the old section contains people whose families have lived in Israel for centuries.

Now the time was late afternoon and we were driving toward the Sea of Galilee where we would be staying in a kibbutz for the night. None of us had any idea what a kibbutz would be like and we were pleasantly surprised to find very comfortable accommodations in motel-like rooms with private baths. We were to stay in this kibbutz for two nights.

The group's meals for breakfast and dinner were in the kibbutz dining room and the food was delicious with most of the vegetables and fruits being grown right on the property.

During the trip the accommodations where we spent the night served our morning and evening meals in their dining room. All the food tasted very good.

Lunches were eaten close to whatever site we were viewing and hearing about. Some of the restaurants served the traditional food of the country, while other places offered an Americanized menu along with the Palestinian one. One local lunch food for which I developed a taste was Falafel. This is a dried vegetable mix formed into little paddies and cooked in oil. Three of the paddies are put into a pita pocket and the each individual can add chopped lettuce, celery, onion, etc., plus a salad sauce. Very tasty!

After a good first night's sleep in the kibbutz we drove a short distance to where Jesus on a hillside overlooking the Sea of Galilee to spoke the beatitudes. The beauty of the surrounding country in itself was inspiring. Then while we sat as a group and with the Pastor reading the beatitudes the hush of reverence came over all of us.

Quietly we filed back into the bus to be taken to the monstrous sized archeological site where much restoration work on the area of Saul's palace was taking place. We wandered around for about an hour stopping where spots of interest were pointed out; where David fled from Saul, where Absalom was killed, where the palace and other buildings sat.

Emotions filling me were of desolation and sadness. Just thinking about what God offered to Saul, yet how he went his own way, and the end result of it.

On the following day the desolation sense came in the morning when we visited the town of Chorazim. We wondered along the paths and into the buildings of a ghost town. Chorazim is now standing exactly as it was at the time of Christ.

When Jesus visited there the town rejected Him and His works. The Son of God committed it to destruction. From those days until today, the people in Israel feel the town is cursed and will not live there.

From Chorazim our travel took us to the palace where King Ahab and the wicked queen Jezebel once lived. She was the one who opposed Elijah and who introduced foreign gods to be worshipped by the Hebrew people. We saw the spot where Jehu commanded two of the queen's eunuchs to throw her off the balcony, and where she landed in front of Jehu to be eaten by dogs.

The morning of viewing God's awful judgment drew to a close and we were back to the kibbutz around two 'o'clock.

The first afternoon site to visit was located in a large building right next to the kibbutz. In the building's entryway we gathered around our guide Peter and he told us about the exceptional item we would be viewing. It seems for the last few years the area has experienced very dry conditions. So dry the Sea has receded several feet.

One morning a few fishermen were walking in the mud along where the sea used to lap the shore and they stumbled over some object down in the mud. Immediately the men started to dig and surprisingly exposed a portion of a very old wooden boat. The men notified the authorities about the find.

Well trained people arrived on the site to try to determine the age of the boat and to see if it could be preserved. The conclusion was the boat was probably about 2000 years old and used for fishing. Once the find was made public the Christian people began to wonder if there was a possibility Jesus ever sat or stood in the boat.

Very carefully the mud was removed from the inside of the boat and from the area around. Then the wood was encased in wax and the structure was brought inside to have the wax removed. An air tight room was constructed and the boat was place in the room.

We all moved to a glass wall through which we saw the large wooden fishing- type boat. In the context of today's boats it appeared to be an extra big row boat. Once again awe descended on our group as we contemplated all the stories the boat could possibly tell.

But the sense of awe for the afternoon was just beginning. Upon leaving the building we walked down a path toward the water's edge to take a boat ride on the Sea of Galilee. When we almost reached the dock there were fishermen examining their nets by the edge of the water. The scene seemed to be the retelling of a Bible story right before our eyes.

Our boat looked like a present day fishing-party boat. The deck was large enough for us to all have a seat and it was covered to protect the passengers from inclement weather. Surprisingly though the captain did not steer it with the round steering wheel we are accustomed to. He used what looked like a wooden lever imbedded in the floor and he faced the back of the boat, not the front.

The Sea was exceptionally calm, but the Captain warned us unexpected fierce gales could come up very quickly in the area. This did not happen while we sailed north past the town of Tiberias and around the Sea and on until we landed back again at the Kibbutz dock. The trip was lovely with warm breezes and lovely sunshine. It was also meaningful as we thought of the disciples fishing on the sea. Or while thinking about Jesus calming storms and His walking on the water.

A quarter of our time in this part of the world was over. We now headed south with our destination being Jerusalem and to use a hotel there as a base for several days. On the way south we stopped at the Jordan river where present day baptisms take place. The banks were lush with wild flowers and there were two groups being baptized in the river water. After a pause to watch the baptism and a walk along the river bank the bus continued on until we reached the Jerusalem by mid-afternoon.

Our hotel sat across from the Government courthouse and offices. The location was perfect for walking to some of the places most Christian tourists want to see. The building was older than the Kibbutz, but very well kept and contained modern conveniences. American style food was served in the dining room.

After settling into our rooms we were taken to the Mount of Olives and Peter told us some of the trees now standing in the garden were in existence at the time of Christ. Olive trees are very hard to destroy and they live for hundreds of years.

Next to the trees sat a lovely church and some from our group wondered into the building just as a Mass started. The priest was telling the people about Jesus leaving the disciples to pray on the mount on Passover night while he went a short distance away to pray. According to the priest, Jesus sat on the rock (imbedded in the alter) to lay His burden before the Father. Then the priest told the people they must do the same thing. They must lay their burdens before the Lord. The words touched my heart and I thought, "How true, how true".

A short distance from the Mount of Olives sat a little Chapel shaped like a tear drop. It is supposed to be the spot where one day Jesus looked over the valley to the city of Jerusalem and wept.

Peter mentioned, "Down below, in the valley both Absalom and Stephen are buried.

I walked inside to sit on a bench and weep. The tears just automatically came as I thought of my Lord's heartbreak over truths He gave to Jerusalem and their rejection of these

COME TRAVELING WITH JUNE

truths; of the future He knew would befall the city, the Temple and His race of people.

This was the second time within an hour tears flowed down my cheeks. The first time was on the mount.

Our group collected together and we walked down a hill which we were told was where the Palm Sunday event took place with Jesus riding a donkey and the people calling out "Hosanna".

The hill was quite steep and underfoot was loose gravel. About halfway down the hill one of the members of the group slipped and fell. Margaret came away with a very large bump on her forehead, but she was determined to not let the fall stop or slow her down.

Almost at the bottom of the incline my right leg started to slide, because of the looseness of the stones. I realized I was going to do a very unlady-like split, so decided maybe if I bent my left knee I would stop the catastrophe. The slide did stop, but where my left knee hit the gravel the slacks gave way into a big tear and the skin over my knee cap rolled up. Ouch!

Onto the bus we climbed and I spent several minutes attempting to clean the wound underneath the rolled flap of skin with wet-wipes and Kleenex while we drove to the gate into Jerusalem. This was Sunday morning and we worshipped in an English speaking Christian church.

After the service our group walked to the Upper Room. One (of the continuous) surprises was to find the tomb of David on the lower floor. The whole building seemed filled with quiet and reverence in the realization of the events which took place in the room.

We strolled out of the building and the first thing to catch my attention was a carving into the stone portal of the next building saying - IN MEMORY OF JOHN AND BETTY STAM. Immediately to my mind came the days of my childhood when in church we would pray for the missionaries

John and Betty Stam. Today the portal is over a school for Hebrew children.

Coleen, the Pastor's wife is a school teacher in Canada. She started up the school's steps to take a peek at the classroom activities, but she only took a few steps and was pursued with a machine gun-toting military man. Evidently visiting a school without special clearance is not allowed in Israel. Coleen quickly changed her mind.

Later in the day we reentered Jerusalem by walking through one of the gates. Like boarding a plane we needed to pass through security before we could go through the portal. One of the things impressed upon us before we did any sightseeing in this city was the importance of a very modest dress code. We were told some times acid was thrown if a person's apparel was not considered proper.

Due to the great time change I woke early most mornings. This new day was no different, and while washing I found some very noticeable dirt under the skin of my knee wound. There seemed to be no other solution than to remove the flap of skin, thoroughly clean all specks out and use a disinfectant. This I did at four a.m.

Later in the day I told two of the ladies about the early morning medical action. Of course the question came, "Didn't it hurt?" My answer, "Of course it hurt." One lady jokingly said, "Oh, I thought the moaning I heard was the Muslim call to prayer. Here it was you." All three of us enjoyed a good laugh at that remark.

Our guide took us to historical sites in Jerusalem during this day. After removing our shoes we went into the Dome of the Rock and found beautiful Mosaic designs on the walls. Imbedded in the center of the huge room is a large rock which is claimed to be the rock where Abraham brought his son to be sacrificed. Of course in the Muslim belief it is Ishmael who is brought to the rock, because he is the first born.

Right out side, and around the corner, of the Dome of the Rock is the Wailing Wall where the Jewish people bring their petitions to Jehovah. We saw many Jewish people standing with their hands on the wall while others stood a few feet away with their hands raised. The men stood at one end of the wall and the women at the other. When we walked close we could see little pieces of paper put in the wall's cracks. These were written prayers. Turning our heads from the wall we saw on the high places around were military men with machine guns who were pacing and watching the ground below.

Now we were to walk the well known Via Dolo Rosa or "Stations of the cross". Before starting up the hill we stepped into one of the lower buildings and were told, "This is where the Roman soldiers waited for orders," and on the floor were markings from the games they played while waiting.

A few doors up the hill we went into another building where we were told the Roman prisoners were scourged. Inside, in the middle of the room, was a thick stone archway with a hole in the center of the top of the arch and a hole about waist high in each of the arch's side walls. Our guide said a rope was passed through the top hole and then passed under the prisoners armpits. The side holes were used to tie the person's hands. They were beaten with whips containing sharp stone pieces.

The steep hill was lined with buildings, some of which noted the Catholic stations of the cross. We paused where it indicated Jesus fell under the weight of the cross. Then at the top of the hill time was spent to explain the fact about crosses being usually located on a road into the city as a warning to travelers of their fate if they commit a crime. Our group also was told the exact way a person was crucified. It seemed the actual death was by asphyxiation. The person was nailed in such a way his lungs could easily collapse and the only way he could fill them with air was by pushing-up his body through pushing on the nailed feet. When a person became exhausted and could no longer push they died.

The last stop for this day was the church over the location the Catholic church claimed was the spot where the crucifixion took place. The entry was through a door in the back of the sanctuary where a priest examined everyone who entered. We were not allowed to carry anything through the door and many of us who were carrying bottles of water were told to leave them.

Down a flight of stairs there was a room with church relics on the walls. We were surprised to see a Muslim man in one corner of the room bowing down in worship because the hour was one of the five times each day a Muslim must bow in worship.

The emotion for much of this day brought tears to my eyes and tears for many others in the group.

Bethlehem, the town of Jesus birth was the destination of our next day. As we rolled along the hills the short distance from Jerusalem to Bethlehem many of us thought of the years long ago when angels appeared to the shepherds right outside of our bus' windows. Lo, not too far from the road, at the crest of one of these hills, what should we see but the very things we were thinking about; a few sheep with a shepherd.

Upon almost entering the town our guide told us about Old Testament Rachel being buried close to Bethlehem. Again the ancientness of what I was seeing struck me.

Of course the town was not at all as I pictured it should be in my mind. The buildings were much more modern and the place was now definitely a tourist attraction with another Catholic structure over the spot where the manger was supposed to have been.

Once again a historic location was underground and we entered the area through a door in the sanctuary, then down a set of stairs. On the lower floor our guide told us about the church being built in a very early century and of some of the historic church events that took place in the building.

Later in the day we visited an olivewood carving shop. The various displays of the work for sale were of an excellent quality. They ranged from large pieces like a communion table to tiny praying hands. I purchased ten of the hands for my grandchildren. Then the beautiful carving in olivewood communion goblets caught my attention and I bought five of them; one for myself and one for each of my four children and their spouses.

Before leaving Jerusalem the next morning our guide told us, "It is a good thing we are going to be away from the city this day. There is going to be a government trial with possible riots expected." The courthouse was across the street from our hotel and if the expected riots took place there was a good possibility they would spread across the street.

About a year before going to Israel I read a novel about Masada and we were going there this day. The novel certainly piqued my interest about the place. The ride south was through barren land and even before we reached Masada the high plateau could be seen from a distance. Once we parked we were given the choice of climbing up the path to the top of the plateau, or else taking the tram up. We all decided the tram was the best way. The trail was steep and the walk would be time consuming.

At the top was what could be considered a good sized fortress. Actually Herod built himself a protected residence there and there were homes, shops and large storage buildings, plus a synagogue.

The horror of the story which took place on this site could be felt as we looked over the wall and saw the remains of the Roman camp down below. All of us imagined the fear plateau residents must have felt as they watched the Roman soldiers (hundreds of feet down) begin to build a ramp to reach and destroy the people living at Masada. What strong determination the Jewish people must have had to decide to take their own lives rather than live in Roman slavery after they were captured. When the ramp almost reached the top of the plateau each husband and father took the life of his wife and children, then his own.

We walked away from what we saw and what we imagined in almost complete silence.

While looking down over the side to the east we saw the Dead Sea; our next stop. Some of our party wanted to go in the water and close to the beach there was a building in which they could change their clothes. It also contained a shopping area and a restaurant.

Years ago I went into the salt lake in Utah and experienced the sensation of being completely buoyant. Once was enough! A few others in our group did not want to go into the water and we browsed the little shop, then enjoyed tea in the restaurant. Several of us walked down to the water to watch those who were floating on top of the sea. Even walking in the sticky, salty, grabbing sand was not pleasant.

Next our bus was off to Qumran and we stopped there long enough to walk to a bluff where we could see the cave in which the Dead Sea scrolls were found.

The day was not complete without a stop in Jericho on our return to Jerusalem. We were reminded by our guide of the story of Zacheus climbing the tree in Jericho and we were taken on an interesting trail through a garden and down stairs into cave-like rooms.

In the center of town camel rides were offered and of course I couldn't resist. At least there was a saddle on the animal's back, but the feat of staying on the creature when it stood or sat took great effort. When a camel stands it gets on its front legs first and the rider is thrown backward. Then, when the back legs stand the rider is thrown forward. Of course the opposite action takes place when the camel sits for the rider to get off. I was so glad to be able to hold onto the seat's knob, otherwise I'm sure there would have been no way for me to stay on.

Our ride back to Jerusalem from Jericho is one I don't believe any of the bus passengers will ever forget. First of all, the road was the original one used at the time of Christ; our Lord walked this road. True, it is paved now, but no wider than it was 2000 years ago. Jericho is below sea level and Jerusalem is hundreds of feet above sea level. The drive was uphill all of the distance, with many switch-back turns and deep ravines on both sides of the road. There were places the front end of the bus went out over the edge of the road with no guard rail in place. Other places the driver needed to back up the greyhound sized bus to make the turn. If I did not have white hair at the beginning of the ride I'm sure I would have had by the end.

About halfway to Jerusalem the driver stopped the bus at a place where we could stretch our legs and catch our breath. We walked to the edge of the cliff for a spectacular view and when we looked across the deep ravine we saw there was a very isolated Monastery high on a bluff. Any man living there would in no way have an opportunity to be a part of the world. Their life consisted of prayer, meditation and whatever trade the Monastery encouraged. No women were allowed.

At the very beginning of our time in Jerusalem Peter warned us about the danger of having our pocket's picked. He said some of the pickpockets were well known and if he saw one coming he would announce, "The birds are coming" in order for us to be on guard. As our bus approached the hotel area Peter said, "There is a bird trying to pick a man's pocket." Of course everyone wanted to see and sure enough, right outside the bus we watched a man's hand enter another man's back pocket and then he ran off with a wallet.

After the very full day all of us were glad to be able to return to our hotel rooms and eat a tasty dinner. Before we went to bed to enjoy a good night's sleep we were informed riots did take place while we were gone. Even though there was now no visible evidence of any riot everyone was glad we were not in the city this day.

Every day so far all of us experienced differing degrees of emotion in what we heard and saw, but during the daylight hours of this last day in Israel proved to be the deepest in heartbreak for me. First we went to the Holocaust Museum and walked through the double rows of trees to honor the Christians who assisted the Jews in Europe to escape from the Nazi regime.

Not knowing what the three buildings contained there was no way to prepare myself for the tears to soon flow freely down my face. The first building contained just a huge open space to express the void, caused by lives lost and it was dedicated to the people, villages and culture exterminated. There was absolute silence as everyone just stood and stared.

Building number two was dedicated to the children who lost their lives. I walked into total darkness and as my eyes acclimated I saw a cylinder of light in the center of the large room. We slowly circled the room, keeping the light on our left and noted on the walls to our right were written names. At the same time over the loudspeaker a voice recited one name after another, with the age of the child at death, and the village they were from. Believe me, my tears were stronger on leaving this building than the previous one.

The third building held a museum containing many of the possessions of the people whose lives were snuffed out. All of us felt the need for an emotional break upon leaving the area where the buildings were located. A cup of tea, a croissant and fellowship around a table helped.

Now, I must make a confession. While we were enjoying our bite of food Colleen mentioned how she enjoyed the chocolate covered croissants she could purchase at home. I determined to try one once I reached Canada. My confession is - I can now blame a Pastor's wife for addicting me to chocolate covered croissants.

During the afternoon we went to the area where Protestants believe the crucifixion could possibly have taken place. There definitely appeared to be the form of a skull on the cliff's face. All of us gathered around and sat close to the cliff to observe communion. Several of us read passages of scripture with lumps in our throats and shared in the bread and wine (served in tiny olivewood cups). We were given the cups as souvenirs.

Peter led us to a tomb at the base of the cliff. No one knows if this was the tomb Jesus laid in, but it was of the type used during Jesus' day. As all dwellings in those days, the ceilings were held up on the inside by rock arches. In the center of the tomb was the arch and on either side were stone slabs where the bodies of family members could be laid. One particular factor in this tomb was the location of one slab where light from the window streamed onto it.

Still the afternoon was not over and we opted to walk through the crowded shops of Jerusalem. The shopkeepers were definitely pushy and determined to sell their wares. Some members of the group did buy some items. Then our guide took us to the restaurant managed by one of his friends for our evening meal. We were served elegant traditional Arab cuisine and most of us enjoyed the variety of flavors different than those found in North America.

This busy day was not finished. We next attended an evening concert of Hebrew songs and dances performed at the YWCA. What a wonderful end to our sojourn in Israel.

Now, for a long day of bus travel from Jerusalem to Cairo, Egypt. We were prepared and advised about the trip by Peter, then given lunch bags to tide-over our hunger until we reached the evening's hotel destination.

Almost as soon as we left Jerusalem the barrenness of the country side became apparent. After riding for a few hours we stopped for a coffee break at a roadside stand close to the Golan Heights.

Outside of the stand were picnic tables where most of us gathered for the break. A few American military men were also at the tables and we chatted. Two of them sat by me and they were most eager to tell about home in the Midwest and about their families.

Both young men were going through the heartbreak of being so far from home for six months and longer. One shared the fact his wife was leaving him and the other longed to see his new born baby at. My heart went out to these young men as I tried to give some encouragement and share some faith. They were just happy to have an English speaking person listening to them.

Shortly before noon the bus reached the border of Egypt and all of us needed to go through the immigration ordeal before us. Actually there were five different stations within the building for us to process through. Each station officer peppered us with questions and then stamped our papers. I was the only American in the group with all the rest being Canadians. There is animosity in Egypt toward Americans and I wondered if I would experience any difficulty at the border, but none appeared.

A different bus awaited for us outside of the immigration office. The Egyptian one was a new Mercedes coach; very luxurious. However the bus could not leave until two more buses filled.

Bus travel in this part of Egypt is with a caravan of three buses containing one armed military truck before the caravan and one behind. This has been necessary for a few years due to some radical Muslim groups attacking tourist buses traveling through the desert area.

Before another hour passed the three buses were filled and we were ready to proceed. At one point we stopped moving (I don't know why) and all of the soldiers surrounded the bus caravan with their machine guns pointing out. When we reached the Suez Canal and were waiting to board the ferry the soldiers performed the same procedure.

For hour upon hour the only thing to see out of the bus' windows were sand dunes and more sand dunes. Every once in a while a Bedouin tent would appear, or a shepherd with his animals, or else a man sitting on a camel. The views our eyes perceived were as if we were being transported back to the land at the time of Christ. The scene would have fit perfectly into any church's Christmas program.

Upon entering Cairo the sight of a multitude of what we would consider tenement housing seemed endless. The buildings were mostly three story, row dwellings with a balcony on the third floor. Wash hanging on the balcony could be seen every- where.

When our Egyptian tour guide joined us the next day he told us the first floor of these houses contained the burial area of the family members with the family's living quarters on the above floors.

Plush is the word best describing the hotel our Cairo stay was in. A beautiful lobby greeted us, with a lovely dining room off to one side in which many tables faced a flower-strewn pool. Three majestic pyramids were within eyesight from the pool's lounge chairs.

My finely decorated room with bath was located on the first floor with a door to exit onto a patio. We were advised never to leave our patio door open and I'm assuming this was to keep any unwanted creatures from entering.

Before leaving home for this tour all of us received a packet of health instructions and advice concerning inoculations.

Most of us followed what was suggested. However one piece of advise stayed in my mind concerning Egypt. This was to avoid stepping in puddles because a deadly parasite is sometimes held in Egypt's puddles. Naturally, with the "keep the door closed" and the parasite advice I wondered what other dangers were also possible.

At breakfast the next morning our Egyptian guide greeted us and gave us a little of the history about his life in Cairo. We found he was a Coptic Christian and the first of this type of Christian faith for most of us to meet.

The Citadel, a renowned fortress in the center of the city of Cairo, was the first place we visited right after breakfast. It is located on a hill and monstrous in size. We were told the Citadel was built early in the period of time when the Crusaders began to conquer sites in Israel. The Egyptian people were determined no Crusader would take Cairo and from the powerful appearance of this place they probably would have been right. However, no Crusader army ever entered Egypt.

In the center of the citadel sat a large Mosque. Again we removed our shoes outside of the building in order to be able to go inside to see all the beautiful ceramic art work. We weren't disappointed.

From the Mosque the distance was short to our next stopping place - the Coptic church; a building much smaller than the Muslim place of worship. Outside of the sanctuary's entrance a map with a specific trail was pasted onto the wall.

One of our group questioned the guide as to the meaning of the map. He replied, "The trail depicts the journey of Mary and Joseph and the baby Jesus." Of course the question followed, "How can you be sure of such a thing?"

Very interestingly our guide responded, "After the death of Jesus there were Christians who came and traveled over the countryside to many towns in order to question the inhabitants if a mother, father and baby passed through at the approximate time the Holy family would be passing through.

Because the fact of a stranger passing through the desolate areas being so very rare it was easy for the people to remember the family. The map was made in the first century."

The guide also told us the apostle Mark came to Egypt to bring Christianity to the people and how the Coptic church is a product of Mark's ministry. He said Mark's body was buried in Cairo.

Later in the day we toured a papyrus factory. First, the papyrus making process was explained and then our time was spent in looking at walls containing beautiful pictures painted onto the papyrus paper. Many of the pictures contained figures wearing Egyptian costumes of centuries ago and the pictures varied in size from those covering a wall to those of a very small miniature.

Only one day remained of this interesting trip. We were up early to travel down to Goshen to view the oldest pyramid in the world. Surprisingly the sides of the pyramid were not smooth like those of the pyramids close to the motel, but this one was built of rounded stones.

Next we went into one of the burial tombs and saw walls adorned with many pictures. The guide told us the pictures depicted the dead person's servants (the images varied in size and shape according to the build of the servant) in order for the person to be served properly in the place of the dead. There were also pictures of family members to keep him/her company.

Three more pyramids were visited. We did not go inside of them as we were told the entry passage was very low and very narrow with no light. If someone in there was trying to come out it would present quite a problem.

Close to these three pyramids sat the sphinx with a platform erected in order for tourists to get a better view. As

I looked at it, all I could think was - what a work of art, how awful for some person to choose to fire a cannon at it (a century ago), and cause such damage to the face.

Early in the afternoon we visited a rug weaving factory. Our first reaction upon entering the building was anger over seeing grade school-age children sitting and working the looms. However the guide explained that the children only worked a half a day and went to school the other half of day to learn the regular subjects. He said, "In actuality the children are better off than many who only attend the grade school because these children will now have a craft from which they could earn a good living." The idea made sense, but then there was also the fact that only tiny fingers could perform the jobs these children were doing.

Our group toured all the floors of the factory and we saw many beautiful rugs being weaved from the small sized throw rugs to large room-size ones. The craftsmen were very congenial and some of them told of learning the craft in this very place when they were children. The rugs sold for thousands of dollars.

Last on the list of sights to see in Cairo was the museum holding all the relics from King Tutankhammon's tomb. Truly he was very wealthy and all the beautiful art work was impressive to look at. One thing was true, even though he took it into the grave with him, he could not take it beyond.

Early the next morning we were on our way to the airport for our flight home. The first leg of the trip from Cairo traveled to Germany and sitting next to me on the plane was a University Professor who taught the Koran. What an interesting conversation we experienced comparing Christian beliefs with Muslim ones. Interesting, but to me also heart-breaking knowledge. Muslims believe Jesus was born of a virgin, He lived a sinless life and He sits now at the right hand of the Father, but they don't believe He is the Son of

God. Jesus is only a prophet in their eyes. My prayer is the Lord will open this professor's eyes.

On arriving at the German airport to change planes we were shocked to learn the computer lost our group of twenty people and there were no seats scheduled on the Air Canada plane for us to fly home. Fortunately, the Lufthansa flight to Vancouver did have open seats and we were on our way, but an hour later then expected.

My longed for trip was over. It was a blessing to be able to see the land where my Lord walked and to see so many of the places written about in scripture. I will never forget the opportunity the Lord allowed me to experience.

FRUSTRATION UPON FRUSTRATION

Ringing in my ears came the words no passenger wants to hear an airline pilot say, "We are running out of gas and must fly to the nearest airport."

How did the plane get into such a predicament? The reason was because we spent the last forty-five minutes circling a California airport due to a disabled Airbus sitting on the runway with all of its tires blown out. This happened just a few minutes before we were to land.

The disabled plane's passengers were waiting for a bus to come from the terminal to unload them. Next, special equipment would arrive to move the huge jet. Once our pilot heard of all this additional delay he knew we needed more gas.

We flew about fifty miles away and on the approach to landing there the pilot announced, "No one is to deplane. We will just remain on this runway until gassed. Then when word comes about the Orange County runway being clear we will leave here."

Once the unscheduled landing took place people's cell phones appeared everywhere and a murmur crescendoed in the cabin. People were phoning and explaining why they would be late. Other people, not on phones, began complaining about being confined to the cabin.

This Alaska Airlines flight turned out to be two hours late reaching its California destination. In the meantime my brother's intention was to pick me up outside of baggage, and he was probably worried.

On reaching the first phone in the airport I dialed my brother's number. Of course no one was home, but I did leave a message concerning my arrival. However, before going outside there was another matter needing my attention.

When first waiting to board the plane I noticed my return ticket was not in the folder and I rushed back to the ticket agent. She insisted she put the return ticket with the folder on the counter and that I lost it. This sounded wrong to me. In all of my previous flights the return ticket was always placed in the folder before being handed back. However, there wasn't time to argue. It was time to board the plane.

At the gate I told the ticket agent of my problem. She told me to report the missing ticket upon arrival at my destination. This was the necessary stop before my walking to the outside curb. Naturally the line to the agent was long and the news not good.

I was informed the departure ticket agent reported the ticket loss was my fault. There were three pages of information for me to fill out to bring with me at my return flight time. Then too, a search fee was required, plus it would also be necessary for me to purchase a return ticket.

All of this stress was on top of the fact that the reason I was in California was to be with my brother for three days as we attended the memorial service for his dear wife's promotion to glory.

My sister-in-law knew and loved the Lord. There was no question about her being with Him, now. When the phone call came to tell me she was released after two years of suffering I did not cry. However, when I thought of my husband welcoming her to heaven and my not being by his side, the tears fell.

106

At the curb, three hours late a familiar car and face pulled to the side to pick me up. The next three days were filled with wonderful family fellowship, plus a beautiful time of remembrance. Yet, all the time there was the dread of the paperwork needing to be filled out. It was taken care of at the very last before returning to the airport.

Arrival at the airport was early because there was no way to know how long the paperwork or the purchase of another ticket would take. This time there was no long line at the ticket counter.

A cheery, smiling agent looked at my name and said, "Oh, we don't need this - we found your ticket stapled to the back of another passenger's ticket." The agent told me when a gentleman arrived at the airport he walked to the ticket counter, and jokingly asked, "Can I use this ticket?" The agent looked at the name of June on the ticket and with a twinkle in her eye responded, "Not unless you are wearing a skirt."

The discomfort of the anticipation of paying for another ticket, the nuisance of filling out three pages of questions, the irritation of the agent's rudeness was all for nothing. The paperwork was handed back to me along with my boarding pass. The only emotion I felt was of rejoicing and praising the Lord. The Almighty took care of the problem and prayers were answered that morning.

SEOUL BOUND

As the plane I occupied taxied out to the runway in Seattle, Washington, the pilot's voice came over the loudspeaker saying, "We must return to the gate because a red light has come on in the cockpit. Hopefully the problem will be taken care of quickly and we will be on our way."

With the problem not being one for mechanics to quickly solve a whole plane load of people milled around while waiting to proceed to their destination. I was supposed to fly to San Francisco to change planes and continue on to Seoul, Korea. As time passed the possibility of making the connection seemed less and less likely.

After waiting about an hour we were informed the plane could not be put into service. However all of the passengers would be assigned on the next flight to their destination. About six of us who needed to make connecting flights out of San Francisco were the first to be reassigned.

Here I learned three other passengers were also continuing on to Seoul and we faced a big problem. According to the schedule we were given, the flight to Seoul would be leaving San Francisco ten minutes before the plane we were on was to land there.

Well into our flight south the flight attendant informed us, "The plane across the Pacific is being held until we board." Then when we touched down an airline employee was waiting at the gate to escort our mad dash across the airport to the overseas gate for Seoul.

I was behind the three younger people sprinting toward the gate, and as soon as I stepped on the plane the door was shut and fastened. It seemed like a sigh of relief passed through the whole cabin as the passengers sensed whatever they were waiting for now finally took place.

Two of this plane's passengers were Gary and Valerie Brumbelow. They were much relieved to see me as they were my traveling companions. Gary and Val lived in the Portland, Oregon area and were supposed to connect with me during the wait time between planes in San Francisco. Concern filled their minds as the waiting time passed and I did not appear.

During this anxious period my own mind kept questioning, "Am I really supposed to be going on this trip?" Then, "If we don't connect should I travel on by myself to Seoul?" My purse contained the ticket to Seoul and one on to Khabarask, Siberia. But there were layovers in both of these cities before going on to our final destination of Yakutsk, Siberia. I knew nothing about the prearranged accommodations at either of the layovers, or how to obtain the ticket to Yakutsk. Needless to say I was much relieved to be on the Seoul connection, and to make the rendezvous with Gary and Val who were sitting in the seats in front of me.

Now I began to wonder if my suitcase made the connection. If it didn't, a small overnight bag with one pair of pajamas, one change of clothing and a cosmetic case were the only possessions traveling with me for a three week trip to Siberia.

When the stewardess walked by I asked her if it was possible for suitcases to make such a quick transfer of planes. She assured me the airline always made sure the suitcases of overseas passengers always accompanied them. I wanted to believe her, but still the uncertainty would creep into my mind off and on.

In Seoul my suitcase could not be found on the baggage carrousel. Fortunately our layover was for almost 24 hours, and when we told the baggage claim agent this fact he assured me my luggage would arrive before we left on the next leg of our journey. He said, "There are two flights due from San Francisco during the next twelve hours." The agent even took the address of the place we would be staying in order to deliver my suitcase there.

Our lodging for the night was at the Yoido church. A short time before we were to travel Gary kept surfing the Internet to see if he could locate a place for us to sleep while in Seoul. He found a Christian church offering rooms to travelers. Although he knew nothing about the church he thought our staying there was a good idea and made our reservations. Later he learned the Yoido church is the largest Christian church in the world.

As our taxi pulled alongside of the church building we were impressed with its magnitude. All of the sleeping quarters were found on the sixth floor of the education building located next to the worship center. We settled ourselves into a comfortable two bedroom and bath suite. From time to time during the evening hours beautiful music was piped into our rooms.

The Yoido church holds seven Sunday services. We rose early and were ready to attend the seven a.m. service. As the three of us approached the sanctuary entrance we saw crowds of people pouring into the building and then learned the only space available for us to sit was up in the third balcony. As we climbed the stairs beautiful music filtered into the stairway.

Awe so filled me from the time I woke this morning through the time I climbed the stairs in the church that there were constant tears brimming in my eyes. Awe over the privilege of going on this trip. Awe over the thrill of attending Yoido church. Awe over the sense of the presence of God.

Because of the tears Val kept asking me if I was all right and I kept assuring her I was. Of course the entire service was in the Korean language. For half of the service we didn't understand the words being said in song or speech, but we did understand they were in praise to God. Then when sermon time came an usher walked to our row and offered us head sets. Located before us, on the back of the pew in front, there were outlets to plug in our sets for translation into several languages. We plugged into the English one and the translation came through clearly.

Following the last hymn a young man approached us and said in English. "My name is John. I spent some time in America for study. Would you like for me to take you sightseeing?"

We did have a few hours before it was necessary for us to leave for the airport and the three of us gladly accepted John's kind offer. First on the agenda was to find a place to eat as none of us took the time to eat before church. John escorted us across the street to a little mall containing a cafe.

We wanted a truly Korean breakfast and John ordered one for us - a bowl of chicken noodle soup and a bowl of rice. Tasty food and good fellowship around a table is hard to beat.

Next John took us for a walk around the streets bordering the church and then into the church's Education building for a tour of all six floors.

After enjoying our time with John the three of us gathered our things and left for the airport. First on my agenda in the airport was to visit baggage claim to find out if my suitcase arrived. The agent informed me, "Oh, yes and we sent it in a van to your lodging."

A sinking filling filled me. Then the agent said. "I'll phone the driver and have him go pick up your suitcase and bring it here. Hopefully it will arrive before your plane leaves."

A half hour later I returned to the baggage desk and there sat my suitcase. Profusely I thanked the agent and at the same time thanked and praised the Lord.

When Gary and Val first realized my suitcase was not in Seoul he told me that if my suitcase did not arrive before we left this city it would never reach me in Yakutsk, Siberia. We just experienced another, "But God!"

DESOLATE

She stood alone in front of one of Seoul, Korea's International Airports. Tears were brimming her eyelids and ready to cascade down her cheeks. Her features clearly defined the fact the woman was not a native of Korea.

Because of my curiosity there was no way I could avoid going up to her. First I asked, "Do you speak English?" Upon the response of, "Yes", the next question bubbled from my mouth - "How can I help you?" Immediately a big problem came tumbling from Sveta's lips. She told how for the last two hours she and her baby (in a coach) waited at this spot for her husband and young daughter to arrive from Seoul's other International Airport.

Earlier in the day the family of four flew in from Moscow, and because they were carrying so much luggage they divided their possessions into two cabs. She and the baby came in one cab, with the husband and daughter supposedly following in the other. But the second cab never arrived. To make the problem even more monstrous, the husband held all of their passports and money.

I was traveling with two companions, Gary and Valerie. As soon as they learned of the problem Gary went into the terminal to find out if it would be possible for an agent to contact the other terminal and have the husband paged. Gary was informed they were not able to do this. The only other alternative seemed to be for Gary, Sveta and her baby to take the shuttle to the other terminal while Val and I stayed with the luggage and baby carriage.

Once the Gary, Sveta and the baby alighted from the shuttle they searched everywhere for the husband and daughter, but could not find them. Again Gary asked about having the man paged, and was told, "We only page for lost children and citizens."

There was nothing left for Gary and Sveta to do but return to us. While traveling back aboard the shuttle they came across a man standing in the middle of the street who was hailing every passing vehicle. It was Sveta's husband. Finally Father, mother and children were together.

Unknown to us there was a third terminal for national flights. This was where the woman and baby were supposed to have been taken. Sveta's cab driver took her to the wrong terminal.

The family of four rushed for their baggage and dashed toward the third terminal in hopes of making their connecting flight. However, I imagine even if they didn't make the flight, the fact they were together was more important than a missed airplane.

Gary, Val and I felt our Lord put us at this airport, at this very time, for an angelic mission.

SIBERIA - FACT AND FICTION

Have you ever endured a broken heart? Perhaps it was caused by someone rejecting your friendship. Or maybe someone you dearly loved died and the hurt you felt was very deep. Have you ever ached when you looked into the eyes of someone without Christ; someone without hope or joy or peace. With the latter thought in mind no Christian who ever travels to Siberia can escape a broken heart. Maybe even a heart beyond being broken. One completely crushed.

All my life I have pictured Siberia as a vast wasteland with very little population. Oh, from time to time I heard there were Christians being sent there by the Communist government. Still my mind pictured a prison located on tundra with no city or village in sight. How blind I was to the truth about the fact there are millions of people living in this part of the Soviet Republic.

About eight years ago InterAct Ministry became aware of a need for missionaries to be placed across the Bering Sea from their work in Alaska. The director of the mission traveled over the sea to find out if such an outreach was feasible. Today there are several InterAct families and some single ladies working in the city of Yakutsk alongside of the Russian "Gospel to the East" mission.

Recently God allowed me to go to this remote area of the world. From Seattle, Washington five days of travel were

115

required to reach Siberia. In Seoul, Korea, on one of the overnight layovers God used the time to prepare me for all I was to see and hear.

Upon awaking in the morning, a sense of God's presence filled me, and I was on my knees in awe of the Almighty, plus the amazement over the privilege of being in this place. I did not realize until the end of my trip how necessary this sense of God's closeness was needed for all I would feel while in Russia.

Three days later when the city of Yakutsk, was reached we were greeted by caring Christian Russian men and four of our missionaries who deposited our party of seven into different homes. My lodging was with the single missionary lady in the home of a Russian woman and her eleven year old son.

Siberia is the land of ice and snow - correct? "Nyet" (no)! This September day the temperature was fifty degrees Fahrenheit, ten degrees Celsius, and there was no ice or snow to be seen. One more concept of mine annulled.

True, the northern section of Siberia is frozen year round, but this central area experiences summers in the ninety degree range, with high humidity and twenty-four hours of sunlight. Gardens grow bountifully because of the intense heat, and every family is entitled to a little plot of land. Potatoes, onions, beets, carrots, squash, zucchini, cabbages and various berries grow well. Those who build hot houses also grow tomatoes, cucumbers and peppers. Families enjoy fresh vegetables during the summer time and home canned ones the rest of the year.

The city of Yakutsk can correctly boast about its lovely harbor located on the mighty Lena River. There are interesting museums to see and a very modern hospital (built by Austria) to visit. Then too, the city contains a renown music school in an area known as "Canada Village", because the Canadian government built the housing for it. Lovely tree-dotted country scenes surround the city.

However, the first sights which caught my eyes were the stark cement apartment buildings. These structures were connected by muddy walkways, pitted with deep puddles, and I learned the mud turned to ice for about six to seven months of the year when the frigid weather arrived.

There were areas where sidewalks existed, but due to the frost heaves the cement became broken and very uneven. Some of the cement contained metal u-shaped hooks on the right and left of each square. These too became ice encrusted in winter.

Walking on gooey mud could be dangerous, but ice would make a foothold doubly dangerous. The two weeks I lived in Siberia I never took my eyes off of where my feet were being placed.

Each cement apartment complex was either five or six stories high, containing approximately 120 of the one, two or three bedroom suites. There were no elevators. These apartments did have electricity, running water and heat. However hallway lighting was minimal and in some places nonexistent. In one of the buildings I walked into pitch blackness and grabbed the railing to walk up the 20 steps to the first floor. At the fifth step the railing disappeared. At this point prayer became very focal in my mind. God did allow me to make it safely up the flight of stairs.

The only other dwelling choice, beside the concrete complexes, are wooden buildings with no running water, or electricity, and they are heated with wood. A good many of these homes are extremely old, making much of the wood rotted.

The next very apparent impression to me became the fact that in this land the government held utter control over the day to day living of everyone. They decided when the heat was turned on in the apartment complexes, and the people living in them experienced no control over the temperature in the rooms. They decided whether water reached the building or not. They decided whether a person could leave the area to visit another part of the country, or depart for another country. Translating Scripture depended on their decisions. On and on what they chose to allow took hold. But what completely blew my mind was the fact the workers in this land did not receive currency in payment for the long hours of toil. They received products.

Before me collected many ideas about how difficult the life for the people living in Siberia must be.

In the home where I stayed the hostess worked ten to twelve hours a day. Then she came home to prepare dinner. What did we do after dinner? We sang praises to God! The apparent joy of all the Siberian Christians I met made me want to scream out, "All Russians must hear God loves them. Despite the difficult circumstances they live with, God can give them contentment."

How privileged I felt being able to fellowship with these dear Christians, to be able to attend two churches in Yakutsk and also one south (about three hours by bus) in another town. On the bus ride when traveling there we passed one of the famous Siberian prisons to which well-known Christians were banished and incarcerated. As I realized this huge cement prison (surrounded by high walls and barbed wire) was one where many brothers and sisters in Christ died, all I could do was inwardly cry, "Oh, God! Oh, God!"

When I began to pen this story I was flying home from Siberia. Yes, my heart was broken over the living conditions. And crushed from the thought that most of the nine hundred thousand people living in the district of Yakutia have never heard one word about The Living God.. Seventy percent of these people are tribal. They have lived in the land for centuries.

The thirty percent who are Russians came from the west and were either banished to Siberia, or else lured there under the pretense of a good paying job. The tribal people are steeped in animism, and the Russian people are products of 70 years of atheism.

What happened to the Christians who were sent to prison there? The majority of them died. Some escaped to another country, and those who were released (following their confinement) returned west to Moscow, or other large cities.

There are over thirty districts in Siberia. More than half of them have absolutely no Gospel witness. Over and over my inner thoughts kept saying, "There are millions of people who have never heard! Is there any question as to the fact there is a great Spiritual void in this north land? But who actually cares? Who is willing to give up the good life in north America to 'Go and Tell?' How will we be able to look into our Lord's eyes through all eternity with the knowledge we were not willing to go? "

"GO GREYHOUND" IS THEIR MOTTO

The mode of transportation baffled me for weeks. Airplane travel was out of the question; Kentucky to Washington State with seven stops along the way would in no way be an economical flight option.

I thought of renting a car. This seemed to be the most sensible solution with the consideration of the amount of luggage being carried. Of course there was a suitcase full of clothes, plus an over night bag, and a suitcase full of materials for display at meetings. With a vehicle I could drive for eight hours, then find a comfortable motel for the night and only need to remove the over night bag from the car's trunk.

However my children did not like the idea of my driving alone in winter weather across prairies and mountains. They were fearful for my safety. But such a concern never entered my mind; probably because, for many years I drove in much snow and ice.

The Greyhound bus line offered a month's pass with unlimited stops for a very reasonable cost. The only drawback was the fact the trip would require my riding five times for twenty-four to twenty-six hours between the stops. Then too, the luggage hauling prospect was not something I looked forward to.

Finally, the week before my travel was to begin I earnestly sought the Lord's guidance. The Almighty gave me the assurance of the bus being the way for me to go.

The morning for my departure from Lexington, Kentucky to Central City, Nebraska dawned clear and crisp. A distinguished driver stepped on the vehicle and announced, "I am former military. There will be no smoking, drinking, drugs or cursing on this bus. If any is detected the bus will be stopped and a police escort will remove you." With that out of the driver's system we drove out of the terminal.

Travel was pleasant. I enjoyed the scenery, then read a book; enjoyed the scenery, then concentrated on word puzzles; enjoyed the scenery then worked on my embroidery.

Between destinations all Greyhound buses stop for a period of five to forty-five minutes every few hours. The shorter stops were for people controlled by nicotine and the longer ones for food breaks. Of course washroom facilities became busy places at these stops. The bus company brags about now having toilet facilities, but its like a moving porta-potty with no sink or water to wash your hands. Most people try to wait until the next stop arrives.

We pulled into Chicago a half-hour before midnight. Before me stretched a two hour layover before I could catch the bus to Nebraska.

Eating a bit of food occupied some of the time, then came one of my favorite activities - people watching. There were people of different sizes, old and young, people of different races, also people of different life-styles and cultures. All were waiting to be transported somewhere in North America. I was surprised over how friendly everyone seemed. Conversation flowed easily with whom ever sat in the next seat.

Upon entering the two a.m. bus, the most dreaded segment of my ride was to begin. From previous bus rides (twenty years ago) I knew sleep would not come as easily as when prone on a bed.. However the bus was not crowded. What a pleasant surprise to be able to spread out over two seats and most of the other passengers were also able to do this.

I "catnapped" until daylight. Then, because my destination would not be reached until noon the catnap procedure continued until about eleven. I felt rested when stepping-off at the bus station close to Central City.

Elsie, a 92 year old woman, and her daughter Dorothy were waiting in the bus terminal for me and my lodging for the next two nights was to be in Elsie's home. This delightful woman still is very active. She teaches two Bible studies each week, she is involved in her church, and she also cares for the three children of a sick neighbor. God certainly continues to bless Elsie with good health and strength.

Dorothy's husband works at Nebraska Christian High School. My purpose for being in this town was to speak the next day in the Chapel service of the school. Upon arriving in Central City I learned I was not speaking in the Chapel, but to seven class- room sessions; four English and three Bible Classes.

Speaking seven times in one day kept me very busy, but I was glad for the more personal contact with the young people who seemed to show a genuine interest in work among tribal people in Canada, Alaska and Siberia.

To visit with Elsie and her family truly proved a blessing to me. To sleep in a bed overnight was wonderful.

The following morning I was off for the second leg of the trip being Central City, Nebraska to Manhattan, Montana. Another over 24 hour jaunt.

This Greyhound segment required a midnight to two a.m. layover in Cheyenne, Wyoming. Again I chatted and listened to the many waiting passengers. Many heartbreaking monologues flowed into my ears during these hours.

The first person who spoke to me was a young woman with an assortment of earrings and a metal object pierced through her tongue. She was on her way to Seattle to find work in the home care industry. The woman's tearful story was about her husband's desertion of the family and leaving her with two little children. She could not care for her children and work at the same time. There was no supporting family around which brought the young woman to the ultimate decision to put her children up for adoption. The children were gone and she was now alone.

Now a Mexican-American man joined me. He placed on the table one of the Tim LaHaye "Left Behind" books. We began to chat about the book and I learned the man was a Christian who was burdened to become a Pastor in a Spanish-speaking church. The next words out of his mouth were about his wife leaving him and taking their thirteen year old son with her. His heartbreak was very evident, but even more than the marriage breakup and the fact he was alone, was the problem of the divorce possibly preventing his being accepted into the ministry.

All through the two hour layover an agitated young woman kept loudly repeating, "I don't know how I got here." She told the whole waiting room the story of being drunk when she climbed onto the bus and somehow she landed in Cheyenne. On she exclaimed, "I don't have any money to travel any place else."

To me, she acted like she was high on something, and I tried to ignore her. But as time went on I started to become concerned, and I went over to her to see if I could get any information about her family.

Those sitting close to her assured me the girl did have some family in the Cheyenne area. She only needed to get in touch with them. However I did not feel good about what was going on. She could easily go with some stranger and be raped, even murdered.

I went to one of the ticket agents and asked if there was a way help could be provided, because the young woman needed protection. The agent's response was "Nothing can be done. The police will not come unless someone witnessed her taking a drug."

My next bus arrived and I left Cheyenne full of concern for the young woman. Later I learned she was only fourteen years of age, which made me all the more uncomfortable.

In Manhattan, Montana lived a dear family who for years have been supporting the ministry God has entrusted to me. It was a delight to relax in their home, to share a video with a room full of guests, and to worship with them on Sunday.

Leg three of my journey traveled from Manhattan, Montana to El Jabel, Colorado. Beginning shortly into the trip this part of the saga contained bus problems. We left Manhattan during the evening hours and traveled about fifty miles toward Cheyenne when the bus engine refused to travel more than 30 m.p.h. So we limped toward the closest destination where we could change busses.

The layover in Cheyenne was lessened, due to the lateness of the bus, but I did have an hour to kill. One thing important for me to do was inquire about the young girl who concerned me the last time I was in this terminal. The ticket agent claimed to know nothing about the problem. I was disappointed to learn nothing, but also relieved, because, if some terrible thing would have happened it would have been known.

Now a young man of Indian heritage came to chat with me. Out of his mouth poured the story of all the trouble he managed to get himself into while living with his mother. Drink was his greatest problem and he feared he would land in jail if he continued staying at home. So he was on his way to live with his brother.

I shared with him the story of my trouble-bound youth, and told him Jesus Christ changed my life. He got up and started walking away while saying, "I don't want to hear that stuff. My aunt all the time tries to tell me the same thing."

A little later, around dinner time, I bought a burrito. Then saw the young man was not eating and before I bit into it I offered him half. At first he refused. The I took a pen knife

124

out and cut the burrito in half. He gulped it down. It broke the ice and he started talking to me again.

One thing I noticed on this trip was the fact some of the bus passengers often carried bags of food with them. Many did not purchase food at the stops. The question came to my mind, can they not afford to buy food? Quite a few of these people travel long distances, surely they must get hungry some time.

My next bus exchange after Cheyenne was Denver. We arrived there late in the afternoon and I was to board the Glenwood Springs bus early in the evening. As the bus pulled out of the Denver terminal snow was falling. The further west we went the thicker the snow fell.

After being on the road for forty-five minutes the driver knew he could not make it through the pass without chains. We were probably stopped for a half hour while the driver put on the chains. Then when he restarted the engine he found himself with the same problem I experienced while traveling on the bus the night before.

We crawled through the pass. Once on the other side we became the Greyhound going at turtle speed until we reached the assigned break stop. In the meantime the bus driver called the terminal with his cell phone to advise them of the problem. He was told to wait at the stop until a replacement bus could arrive.

About 45 minutes later the new bus pulled into the stop. After all the luggage was transferred and the passengers were seated on the second bus the driver told us it would be necessary for us to wait longer before we could proceed.

The next thing we knew we were surrounded with flashing lights from three police cars. The officers came aboard and pulled five passengers from the rear of the bus.

What every bus driver warned us of was now taking place. Someone in the back of the bus noticed these people were either drinking, or using drugs and reported it to the driver.

Before our eyes the police questioned and body-searched the five. Two were allowed to return to the bus. The other three were put in the police cars and driven away.

The time was now after 9:30 p.m. and there were still hours to ride before reaching my destination. Nine-thirty was the time I was supposed to have arrived in Glenwood Springs, where my prayer partners waited for me. The only alternative for me was to phone them and advise them I would call whenever I arrived. Of course they were not at home to receive my call. They were at the bus terminal, but I was able to leave a message and I knew they would return home and receive it before my bus pulled into Glenwood Springs.

The arrival time to my destination was 1:30 a.m. and the terminal was closed and in darkness, but fortunately there was a phone outside. My prayer partner said he would pick me up in fifteen minutes.

For the second time during this trip I enjoyed a visit with people who for almost 30 years were involved with praying for and supporting - first the Temple family, then my hubby and I. Now my ministry alone.

There was chatter about old times and what was presently taking place in our lives. I carried with me family pictures and pictures from my Siberia trip, plus two mission videos on the Alaskan and the Siberian work.

Quickly time went by and I found myself on a short jaunt back to Denver to spend the weekend with son David, his wife Arnette and grandchildren Josh and Laura. It is a special bonus for me to be able to visit with loved family members in so many areas of the states when I'm either traveling to or coming from meetings.

Yet still before me were two more overnight hauls before my final destination would be reached. The next one left Denver (with snow falling) early in the evening. The bus was crowded and there was no hope of being able to partially stretch out over two seats.

The last person to be seated was the bus driver. But before he sat he announced, "Please stay in your seats tonight, unless you need to use the rest room. Between Denver and Pocatello, Idaho there are numerous elk herds. They often cross the road at night and there is a good possibility I will need to jam on the breaks every so often."

He was right! Time after time jolting stops occurred because out of the pitch- blackness on the right hand side of the road a dozen or more elk would leap into the bus' headlights. Thankfully the driver was able to keep from hitting them, and they were majestic to watch.

The driver later told us, "Once in a while it is impossible to miss an elk. I always feel bad when I hit one."

In Pocatello, lived a couple whom I have known for thirty years. They worked at a Christian camp where two of my children worked for two summers. We have kept in touch ever since. Seeing them again, plus being able to bring them up to date on the mission's activities was a blessing to me.

Pocatello was only a day stop for me. At eleven p.m. I boarded the bus to take me to Grangeville, Idaho. The distance on the map didn't look like Grangeville was more than a six or eight hour drive from Pocatello. However, going by bus we were routed north to Butte, Montana, then west to Spokane, Washington, and finally south to Grangeville.

I exchanged buses in Butte at one a.m., and when I stepped on the bus to go west the man sitting in the first seat on the right hand side said, "Here, you can sit next to me." I didn't know if I wanted to sit next to him, so I continued walking toward the back of the bus. In seat after seat the people were sleeping. There were no empty ones.

Upon returning to the front row seat the man and I chatted for a while. I learned the man was excited about going to Seattle to attend the wedding of a daughter whom he had not seen for 23 years. Before he fell asleep I knew all about his present life; where he lived and with whom he lived.

At three a.m. the bus driver began telling me his sad story concerning an unfaithful wife who ran away with his best friend. She returned to live with the bus driver, but life is difficult and children are involved. I tried to keep assuring him how forgiveness helps to ease the hurts. There was no sleep from me this night.

Snow began to fall heavily when we stopped at a restaurant for breakfast at eight a.m. Here we learned we were stranded, because the mountain pass before us was closed due to the large amount of snow. Four hours later the pass was open and we continued on. My seat partner was very relieved, because the longer we were stranded the more concerned he became over the possibility of missing his daughter's wedding. If all went well from now on, he would be able to arrive in Seattle on time.

Of course we arrived in Spokane much later than expected and my bus south departed two hours before I arrived. The next one would not leave for two more hours, but because of the heavy snow it would only travel as far as Lewiston (an hour north of Grangeville).

Immediately I found a phone and called the Pastor in Grangeville to let him know what was going on. The Pastor advised me to take the bus to Lewiston. He would call friends in Lewiston and they would meet me. From all indications the road to Grangeville would be open on Saturday and I could take the morning bus down.

All did go well and I spent a lovely time with new-found friends. There was not much time to chat when I arrived late Friday evening, but the next morning around the breakfast table, we were able to converse and come to know each other.

The ride south was in sunshine, and all day the snow kept melting. Then at night the temperature turned frigid and on Sunday morning before our eyes lay a sea of ice. The first thought which came to my mind was, "What shall

I put on my feet?" Being the speaker for the morning there was no other option but to slide to church somehow.

When I stepped out of the car in front of the church I felt like a hippie of yester-year. There I stood in a skirt almost to my ankles and on my feet were Nikkei walking shoes. My dress shoes were in my right hand and the Pastor held my left arm.

We took three steps, then my right foot slid to the right. With the next step the left foot slid to the left. The pattern continued, but fortunately there were only a few steps to the church door and we did manage to achieve our objective without landing in a tangled mess on the ground. All I wanted to do was giggle over the ridiculous sight we must have been.

During the time I was speaking I was struck with the awesomeness of how God prepared hearts to hear about His work in northern regions; a field of ministry not usually heard about. There was much interest from the members of this church's congregation.

Monday afternoon included a short jaunt back to Spokane to visit with two more prayer partners. They arranged for friends to come to lunch the next day to hear about the work of InterAct Ministries.

Now I boarded the bus for my last ride on the bus pass. It was just a day trip to take me to Seattle in time to celebrate the Christmas holiday with my family living there.

Through three weeks of travel the hand of the Lord rested on me. All the time I felt the peace, the joy and the safety only the Almighty is able to provide.

One afterthought which often pops into my head when the trip comes to mind is the fact there really ought to be a Greyhound ministry to meet the needs of all the hurting people traveling by bus.

PURELY FUN

After the major part of my year being spent on the road for speaking engagements and meetings, the next six weeks planned were to be purely family fun. Of course, with children living miles apart the first leg of my trip needed to be traveled by plane from Seattle, Washington to Denver, Colorado to attend the high school graduation of my grandson Joshua.

A few years of my life have passed since I've been to a grandchild's graduation. For the six previous graduations I attended, the schedule contained an attendance at the Baccalaureate Service and a Commencement Ceremony, plus a dinner in honor of the student. Several of the schools held an all night supervised party for the students. Now, there are still these scheduled occasions, but the real name of the game is party, party, party.

Not only the graduates themselves attend the party, but brothers, sisters, parents, grandparents, aunts and uncles are all caught up in the whirl of visiting and eating. I became addicted to meeting new people, chatting and enjoying food.

The ceremony for Josh's graduation was held in Denver's picturesque Red Rocks Amphitheater. High above the city sat this engineering feat of the nineteen-forties. It was chipped, hacked and blown out of solid rock. The roof became the open sky, three walls were cascades of stone and a fourth wall did not exist. In its place was a view for miles and miles of countryside. There could not be a more magnificent place to hold special programs.

Josh's party followed the ceremony. His parents and his friend Matt's parents joined together for the event and its preparation.

Matt's and his folks live on a ranch and they chose to have the party in the barn. For the entire day before the two boys graduation they and their fathers cleaned the barn. Then decorated and set up enough tables to hold the 75 to 100 people who would be in attendance for the barbecue party.

Of course the ladies were occupied with food preparation. My daughter-in-law Arnette's particular job was making the cake. When you live 8000 feet above sea level it becomes a real art to adjust the ingredients correctly in order to prevent the cake from falling when it is taken out of the oven.

Arnette wonderfully succeeded in the ingredient adjustment. The next difficulty came in moving the two layers from the cooling position to the icing position. At certain points four hands were necessary to prevent the layers from breaking apart. The finished product became a work of art and quite a "hit" at the party. In my opinion none of the other Denver parties could match the barn barbecue.

After making the reservations to fly to Denver I compared the cost of flying from Denver to Lexington, Kentucky with the cost of going by bus. There was no comparison. The airlines wanted hundreds of dollars, while the bus, with the early purchase discount, only charged $79. The bus ticket was purchased before I left Seattle.

My departure from Denver was scheduled for eleven in the morning on June 5th, and I was to arrive in Lexington on the next day at nine in the evening; a thirty-four hour ride.

All went well until the bus reached 50 miles west of Chicago. There it broke down and we sat along the side of the freeway for two hours before another bus traveling to

Chicago came along. It stopped and there were enough seats empty to hold everyone but three of the passengers. Three men chose to stand in the isle, holding on to chair backs rather than being left behind.

Everyone on the list to make a connecting bus missed it. During the time the ticket agents spent straightening out the mess we bus passengers sat around and chatted. I met a man from Ethiopia who was headed east, a woman from Mongolia going south, and Americans going north, east and south. Despite differing cultures and customs we were like one friendly family, having all been placed in the same situation.

At last I was seated on a bus to Indianapolis where there would be one more layover before catching my last bus going southeast. My arrival time in Lexington would now be at five a.m.; eight hours later than originally expected.

A tall good looking young man also climbed on board the bus. There were five seats for him to choose from and he decided to sit next to me. I guess I looked like a well padded grandmom to lean against during his attempted night's sleep, and that is exactly what happened. With the road's curves the young man's long legs either flopped out into the aisle or back against his surrogate grandmom. So also went his shoulders while sleep enveloped him.

My five a.m. arrival was a day later than expected and on the morning of Lauren's graduation party. The household would soon be a buzz for the evening event, but for now the house was calm. I was able to catch up on some of my lost sleep (for a few hours).

Lauren's party was in the form of an open house. Naturally, my daughter-in-law Bonnie and both granddaughters kept busy all day with cleaning and food preparation. During the evening hours the house filled and emptied with people several times. Like Josh's party about 100 people were fed and there was much fellowship. The party proved to be a big success.

On graduation day (the first Saturday in June) plus the following day we did not eat one meal at home. Breakfast, lunch and dinner were all at the party times of Lauren's graduating friends.

The meaningful ceremony of the graduation itself was held in the huge gymnasium of the University of Kentucky. Then in the evening came the great "lock-in" party held at the school. Because both my son and his wife were involved with the activities at the party I was invited to come along. My eyes were opened to all the preparation planning and fun arranged for the students.

In every hall and many of the classrooms on the school's first floor something was going on. It ranged from the dunking tank for a teacher to bean bag tosses, to the dance and snacks in the dining hall, and on and on. I saw first hand how the students enjoyed all the "drink-free" enjoyment.

Following all the party times my family fun did not end. Charles and Bonnie's 25th wedding anniversary celebration came in the form of a cruise to be held at the end of June.

Once more I made an over night bus trip. This one from Lexington to Miami, Florida, from where the cruise ship left. All went well, and I even was able to use two seats on the night time leg of travel.

The next seven days became filled with ideal holiday enjoyment and abundant good food. When we were sailing there were all the various shipboard activities to keep us busy. When we were on land we became beach and water bums.

My six weeks of relaxation drew to a close with the flight from Miami to Seattle. I came home energized and ready to plunge back into ministry, and also filled with wonderful memories. The words of the chorus of an old hymn kept popping into my mind - "Precious memories, how they linger, How they ever flood my soul; In the stillness of the midnight, Precious, sacred scenes unfold.

I cannot help but feel blessed with all the wonderful memories of a life with my children and grandchildren.

DAYS OF YORE

The southern life style, beautiful plantations and Civil War history becomes alive when traveling through Mississippi and Louisiana. Annetta and I were on a summer visit to see and understand all we could about life in the mid-eighteen hundreds, and to view the mighty Mississippi river.

With our departure point being mid-Kentucky we naturally first stopped at the historical homes of Abraham Lincoln before pressing on to the first planned stop of Vicksburg. In the late afternoon our car approached the outskirts of the city and before doing anything else we drove to the banks of the mighty Mississippi to watch the flow of the massive volume of water.

We spent all of this afternoon driving through heavy rain. Now the clear sky and lovely river scene brought a sense of contentment. Then the thoughts came about the river being just as lovely on sparkling clear days during the eighteen-sixties, but entrenched in the area were two armies; one was dressed in blue and the other in gray.

For eight months skirmish after skirmish followed with the Union army attempting to capture the Vicksburg stronghold. Finally on July forth (a day after the Gettysburg battle) the last major battle of the war took place with Vicksburg falling. The south was defeated.

Today the entire battlefield is a National Memorial. Annetta and I drove around the time honored place. Every few feet on both sides of the road were markers honoring divisions or individuals who served in either the Northern or Southern army.

One of the largest memorials is a building containing the names of all the men who served with Illinois battalion.

We stopped and walked inside to see the walls completely covered from floor to ceiling with the names of men placed within their divisions. One of the names was John Barnett, my great grandfather. This was something I never expected to see and came upon it purely by accident. The impact put me into thankfulness over the fact he was not one of the 17,000 men buried on the grounds.

With Plantation hopping being the motto for this trip we next drove around Vicksburg in order to slowly cruise past their stately mansions; ooh-ing, aah-ing and pointing out ones particularly catching our attention.

Then on we traveled southward to connect with the Natchez Trace Parkway. However, because the time was noon before we even left Vicksburg it was necessary to shortly leave the main road to find a place to eat. Into the delightful little town of Port Gibson we drove.

On a side street we found a small antique shop with a sign stating, "Lunch Being Served." In we went to find only four or five tables in what was once the houses' living room. The atmosphere with antiques surrounding us proved unique, and the only one lunch choice they served was tasty.

Naturally, before leaving the shop it was necessary to inquire where we would find the oldest buildings. We learned the oldest Synagogue in the south was located on the main street and it became our first stop. The building was no longer in use and it was locked. We peeked in windows, then drove on to the streets containing the older homes.

Back to the Natchez Trace Parkway we went to again face an afternoon of extremely heavy rain. It ceased as the city of Natchez came into view. Little did we know this would be the pattern for the entire trip. We were thankful though for the fact the rain fell only when we were driving from town to town, or during the night time hours, not when we were actually sightseeing.

Natchez contains many beautiful old heritage homes and some of them are open to the public. Before our trip Annetta spent time researching information on the southern plantations and located a special one in this city called "Auburn". This home was built in 1812 for the first Attorney General of the Mississippi territory, the honorable Lyman G. Harding.

Upon turning into the driveway the stately old elm trees on the property gave the large brick home a special elegance and, as with many of the old plantation houses, the white columns at the entryway catch one's attention before anything else. Auburn, with the architecture being completely of brick construction gave the home an authentic colonial American look. Our eyes glided across the expansive house in appreciation.

One of the home's unusual interior features we found located right in the foyer as there stood a unique free standing spiral staircase. The two of us stopped in our tracks to stare. While we were gawking at the staircase a pleasant receptionist joined us to offer a guided tour through the building.

The gracious guide took us through each room on the first floor while explaining the purpose of the room, the people who lived in the home and the life style of the century they lived in.

When it was time to go upstairs we used a stairway in another area of the house, not the spiral one. What caught my attention more than any other object was located on the second floor. Despite all the lovely furniture and the interesting lives of the occupants my eyes riveted to a portrait of a lovely young woman. When the guide saw my interest in the picture she told us the portrait was of a young family member, who was preparing to go overseas as a missionary, but never attained her goal. She met her death in an accident.

How my heart ached for the family. They must have wondered, "Why, God, why? This child was preparing to serve you and her life was cut short."

Of course it is impossible for us to know the purpose of God allowing this young woman's life to be taken; we can only speculate. Perhaps the death was with the purpose to make more Christians realize the fact that there are people in the world who will now never hear about the love of God because this young woman could not go. Could they themselves have been given the desire to go and tell in her place?

Whatever the reason, the young woman herself is now in a heavenly place with the Saviour she loved. Death was gain for her.

Once again the time was near noon when we pulled away from a National Landmark onto a highway to travel south. In a short while hunger was felt and we drove off into another small town to find a place to eat.

This was a smaller town than the one we found the day before. The downtown was just one block long and there was only one place serving food. Annetta and I were the only customers. There was also a sense we were not wanted, the feeling was especially strong from one of the servers.

We ate quickly and left. Afterward I wondered about the possibility of there being a color bigotry. All of the people around us were black and our skin was definitely not that color. Or was it due to a bigotry toward strangers? Whatever the cause, the feeling was certainly uncomfortable.

Within a few hours we arrived in Creole country. Our desire was to travel to Houma, one of Louisiana's southern-most towns. But Houma would take another day of driving, so we stopped around five o'clock to spend the night in a motel in a town called Lafayette.

Creole country demanded Creole food. The motel receptionist recommended the favorite restaurant in town and when we drove to the location we found we were at a gas station. Annetta and I were not sure we wanted to eat there. However there were many cars parked around the station, so we know something was attracting customers.

In we walked to be ushered through the station and into a large dining room. Everywhere people sat with huge plates piled high with crayfish in front of them. Neither one of the two of us felt brave enough to try the Creole delicacy the other people were consuming, but we did order other sea food dishes native to the area and thoroughly enjoyed what we were served.

My curiosity over how the crayfish were eaten could not be contained. Before leaving the restaurant I asked a person with a contented look on his face how he went about removing the shell in order to eat the meat. The next time I visit a restaurant serving Crayfish I'll know to break the tail off, pull the flesh from the shell and dip it in the sauce before eating.

The best description for the next day of travel would be rain, heavy rain and heavier rain. By the time we reached Houma the skies were pouring buckets of water. We drove around the town, but the weather kept us from seeing much.

During the evening in the motel room the TV screen kept flashing "flash flood warning". I picked the phone up to call the desk to find out if there was any flooding possible in the motel area. The phone was dead.

Thinking the dead phone should be reported I went outside and walked to the motel entrance. Fortunately for me the walkway was covered because the rain kept violently descending.

The motel clerk informed me they always turned the phone system off when a storm's electricity filled the air. Full realization of the amount of electricity flying around struck me while going back to my room. Streaks of it kept attacking poles just 50 feet from where I walked. All I could do was cry, "Oh, God protect me!" and the Almighty did allow me to reach the safety of my room. I also realized how ignorant I was over the violence of such an electrical storm, since I never before experienced such a severe one.

Our focus on this day was to tour Laura's Plantation on the river road close to Vacherie. The drive was just a short distance from Houmas and in every direction we could see large amounts of water sitting in the surrounding fields. On the approach to the main road it became necessary to drive through a very deep puddle. But once we were on the main road the drainage was better and we reached Laura's Creole Plantation well before noon.

As the two of us approached the property we could see a large home with a lovely front yard, but the house itself was not built in the style of the other plantations we visited. There were no large white front pillars. However, while the architecture was different the home still remained very impressive.

The house itself sat on pillars. On walking through the pillars we saw a large wine cellar. There were no stairs from it going up to the living quarters and this made the wine cellar only accessible from the ground.

A guide, with a group of about fifteen people, led us up a grand double staircase from the ground to a verandah across the entire front of the house. There were three large rooms on the first floor; a kitchen, a dining room and a parlor, with the entryway to each of these rooms accessible only from the back outside porch or verandah in the front. There were no inner connecting doors between the rooms. Nor was there an inner stairway to the upper floor. We needed

139

to walk out onto the back porch to get to the stairway and then found the upper floor contained a parlor and the bedrooms.

While the guide was taking us through the rooms she pointed out the resplendent authentic furniture and told us interesting stories about the people who lived on the plantation.

Laura Desiree Archinard Lacoul was the daughter of the original plantation owner and one of his slave women. As a young woman she married and the plantation was then passed on through her to her children and grandchildren. Presently it rests in the hands of the National Register.

When Laura lived she passed a ruling saying, "If you do not work you cannot live in this house." So when Laura reached an age where she was no longer capable of doing much work she built herself a good sized home next to the main plantation. The new home's main feature was a balcony (the length of the building) where Laura would sit to observe everything going on around the grounds.

Laura also passed a ruling concerning language use. If a person could not speak French they were not allowed to visit or conduct business in the main house. They could only meet in a room in a small back building.

During the years the plantation produced crops the slave quarters were located around two miles from the main house. The slaves worked the many, many acres of fields.

From these small slave cabins were written the African tales we today know as "Br'er Rabbit."

Laura's Plantation proved to us to be a very worthwhile stop on this southern tour. The place was unique in the history of our country. Also poignant as we saw and thought about the Louisiana life-style in the early eighteen hundreds.

Annetta and I looked forward to only one more day of sightseeing before we started north to Kentucky. This last day was spent in the city of New Orleans. We drove along Bourbon street and around the city's down town section. Then to the French quarter where we stopped at a sidewalk Cafe.

Annetta (several years before) visited New Orleans and became delighted with this particular eating place. It became a "must see" spot to introduce me to their Biegnets and tea. I am so glad Annetta insisted we stop.

The French crueler-type food was delicious and the taste alone worth the drive south. The early afternoon hours allowed one more look at the mighty Mississippi, one more drive past lovely old New Orleans homes before our approaching the freeway east.

Southern bayous were driven over before the freeway reached the Gulf of Mexico where we came to the town of Biloxi. Of course we could not proceed without a few minutes at the home of Jefferson Davies, but now there could be no more stops, except to sleep, or Annetta would miss her plane home.

Enjoyable days with a friend are one of life's most valuable experiences anyone can have.

ELDERHOSTELS

Bermuda

Two years before my hubby died we were able to enjoy a cruise to Bermuda and found the island enchanting with lovely flowers, pastel colored houses with white tile roofs and unique sounding birds. The trip was a 45th anniversary honeymoon.

Several years later I was given another opportunity to visit the island. This time was with an Elderhostel group to study the history of the island, plus some lessons on oceanography.

For lodging we stayed at the Oceanographic College and for two days spent time on the ocean learning about plankton and sea life.

The history professor was excellent. We learned the island's towns came into being due to a shipwreck in the early 1600 and we studied what life was like for those stranded people. A most amazing fact was how they managed to rebuild their ship and a year later reach their destination of the new world.

One other reason urged me to visit Bermuda. I wanted to do some research on stories I heard about captured North American Indians being captured in the early 1800's and being taken as slaves to the island.

Each free afternoon I went to St. George's library and dug out facts. Yes, warring New England Natives were captured and put on British ships to be transported to Bermuda. Once there they became slaves on the whaling ships, or for any other capacity they could fill.

Then I found an interesting fact about how they were treated. Because the Indians were constantly fighting among themselves, or with other slaves, or trying to escape, the island's government officials and slave owners met to determine what would be the best way to counteract the violence. An unwritten law was passed to the effect that a North American Indian could only marry a docile black slave. The slave owners believed the docility would counteract their violent tendency. The law was strictly enforced and intermarriages took place. However the Indian people would not give up their culture and did not want to be called a Bermudan.

One evening during the course some of the island's Native people were brought to the college to perform island dancing. This dance group's facial features looked like those of an American Native, but their skin was much darker, and the dance steps were the same as those I've seen on reservations in the United States.

Research brought me to the conclusion that today most of Bermuda's Indians live on the southern island of St. George's. The last afternoon of free time I took the bus to the southern island in hopes of getting more information.

First the idea came perhaps I could gather some information in the bar and in I went. First time in my life I ever walked into a bar and nonchalantly strolled up to the counter, sat, and ordered a coke. The bar tender and I chatted and she recommended I go see one of the old Indians for more information.

Next I went to the village's Evangelical Church to chat with the Pastor. He told me seventy percent of his congregation were of Indian heritage and they even once a year held a Conference with Natives coming all the way from the United States.

This news was most encouraging and a blessing to me in finding a good many Indians on this small island are now Christians despite their sad slave history.

Salem

Early American history began around the town of Salem, Massachusetts. Now my daughter Pauline and I were traveling to this location to learn all we could about the people and the conditions they lived in almost four hundred years ago. We would be taking an Elderhostel course being given on the college campus in Salem.

During the classes we learned much about the Quaker people and their life in this New England town. Learned about the witch trials and visited an Indian village, Plymouth Rock and saw the Mayflower ship. Of course the well known House of Seven Gables (written about in a book by Nathanial Hawthorne) was a place of study one afternoon. Some afternoons were free to do sight seeing on our own or to do research.

One of my husband's ancestors, Abraham Temple, was one of the first people arriving in Salem from England. Pauline and I wanted to see if we could find any particular information on him. Sure enough in the archeological section of the library we were able to find information about Abraham Temple.

When Abraham landed he was deeded five acres of land by the crown. The next year he was given five more acres of land and on the third year he was given a half acre of marshland. If we had not taken the course we would have wondered what anyone would have wanted with marshland. However one of our lessons explained how valuable owning marsh was due to the salt that was extracted from it for home use and for sale.

Abraham was not listed in the records for his fourth year in the new world. From all indications he probably moved away to the Long Beach area of New York as that was where the next research took us.

On the last afternoon free time Pauline and I took the bus down to Boston to see the sights there. Several years before my hubby and I spent a few days in Boston and at that time we found a Temple pew in the old North Church. Naturally, I wanted Pauline to see the church and the pew as well as see other Boston sites.

Captain Temple occupied the North Church pew during the American Revolution and was probably a distant cousin to my husband's.

Our intention upon arriving back in Salem was to go rent a car for the use of taking us to the airport the next morning. The car rental place was about two miles from the bus stop and we walked the distance to learn we were fifteen minutes past their closing time. No one was around and this meant we needed to walk back to the bus stop to get a bus out to the college. It also meant we did not have a car to take us to the airport.

Fortunately we were able to phone a airport service vehicle company in the evening and arrange for our transportation the next morning.

Both of us enjoyed the fun and interesting course. Maybe some day a historical novel will be the result of the Temple Family research done in Salem.

ANOTHER "DAY OF INFAMY"

Where was June Temple on the morning of September eleventh? Naturally, at seven a.m. I was in an airport waiting to board a plane. Daughter Pauline and I watched the terrible events of New York, Washington and Pennsylvania unfold on a TV screen in the food court. Then we noticed the food stalls were closing down and security gates were being pulled across them.

When we asked about our 9:45 a.m. flight the agent told us the delayed departure time would probably be around noon. There was nothing for us to do but sit and attempt to relax.

Next the halls and the ceiling lights were turned off and the two of us went to sit by windows. We watched as one by one each plane was pulled away from the gate and either put into a hanger, or out on the tarmac, a distance away from the airport building.

Our departure time once more was rescheduled to possibly six p.m. Security was everywhere. For three hours we sat, then found out there would be no flights leaving on the eleventh of September. Pauline and I realized two problems faced us. 1. Acquiring our checked-in luggage 2. How to leave the airport area with luggage when no vehicles were allowed on the airport drive.

The first problem was simple. A security agent told us our bags were in the main terminal's luggage area, because all of the planes were unloaded before being put into the hangers.

To reach the main terminal from the overseas satellite the two of us needed to ride the underground train and for the entire time we were riding my mind kept thinking about how terrible a place this would be if the airport was attacked.

We were not stuck in the train and the acquiring of our luggage was no problem. Next Pauline phoned her son Bryon and asked him to meet us in a restaurant out on the highway by the airport. Fortunately, today's suitcases have wheels and all we needed to do was pull them out the driveway to the restaurant.

The events we saw were horrible. Our disappointment in not being able to travel on a long planned trip was depressing. However throughout the entire day the words of a hymn kept popping into my head. I would find myself either humming, or softly singing "When I survey the Wondrous Cross."

Why that hymn? The only reason I can think of is to re-enforce the fact of God's overwhelming love despite any circumstance I found myself in.

AFTERMATH

Air travel became uninviting to many people after 9-11, and I felt fortunate in having already scheduled my meetings within driving distance of my home. However in December it became necessary for me to fly from Seattle to Denver.

By now the public was well informed as to the added security posted in airports and the need to arrive two hours before a flight time because of the security checks before boarding a plane. I followed the requirements.

What was printed was true, in that many more security people were everywhere in the airport. This was more assuring than objectionable, however the long lines to check in and to go through security were not pleasant.

In previous flights, if I had a long wait before flying, or when changing planes, I would often work on some embroidery. This was no longer possible because to have a needle or a small pair of scissors was no longer allowed in the carry-on case. So the hand work now needed to go in the check-in luggage and I would have to content myself with people-watching, or doing a puzzle, or reading (a small price to pay for security) to fill the time.

After a few times of being left-off early at the airport I decided not to check-in my bags for an hour and to sit by the ticket area to do some embroidery. Within a few minutes a security lady came and stood by me. We chatted while I worked away. I learned she was from India and one of her sons was living in America. Two more sons were over in India and she hoped to bring them to America. She was a Hindu. After about twenty minutes of chatting she walked away.

Immediately a gentleman walked up to me and with a very distinct Mexican accent started telling me his story. The man, three hours earlier, debarked from a plane coming from San Diego where he was visiting with his mother and had been waiting all the time for his son to come pick him up. The son lived several hours east of the airport.

Time for me to check in was imminent and I wished the man well before taking my baggage to the counter.

After a couple of trips the actual time of going through the security inspection did not seem much longer than before in the airports where each airline has their own inspection area. Although on one trip I was wearing a new watch and it beeped when I went through the portal. I was pulled aside and inspected with the wand head to toe, front to back, side to side. Then the guard did a hand inspection covering all parts of my body. Finally, my shoes were removed and ex-rayed and the wand did the feet. I felt rather silly standing at the side with my arms out stretched while the female guard went through the whole routine and it was a good thing there was plenty of time to make my flight.

Some airports have only one inspection area for all of their airlines and passenger lines are long when the airport is a large one. In this case a person really needs two hours to get from where they check their bags-in to the departure gate.

After four flights in six months the assurance of safety returned and the new pre-boarding procedures were learned. Then my life once again became busy with air travel to meetings and family visits.

SPAIN

The flying time from Seattle, Washington to Philadelphia, Pennsylvania to Madrid, Spain is extremely long; hours upon hours, twelve to be exact. Two of us made the trip to Spain, however it was in Philadelphia my granddaughter Jessica joined me because her departure point was from Cincinnati.

Jessica is a college senior and her minor is Spanish. The month of March brings a spring break at many colleges and it is the perfect time to take a graduation gift trip. Spain seemed an ideal spot for someone who was fluent in the language of the people.

We arrived in Madrid at 9:30 a.m. to join a bus tour for a trip around the country. Our first get together with everyone was not scheduled until 6:30 in the evening because people would be arriving on different flights all day long.

Jessica and I checked into our rooms in the hotel and then went for a walk around the hotel neighborhood. With the sun shining and the temperature in the mid-fifties (F.) we passed many small shops and a restaurant. Also noted was a Pizza Hut, a Subway Shop and a Burger King nestled among the Spanish stores.

Being the afternoon, almost all of the shops were closed, or were in the process of closing, because it was siesta time. Spaniards usually work from nine a.m. until two p.m. Then take a nap before again opening their places of business around four-thirty or five p.m. and work until eight or nine at night.

The two of us having been on a plane for many hours (with little sleep) and with the time now being 24 hours since we left home we decided it would be best to return to our room to relax and freshen up for the evening.

At the tour group's meeting time we gathered in one of the Hotel's lounges. Jessica and I were among 37 other people, most of whom were from the United States. There was one couple from Canada, a man from Ireland, and a lady from Australia. Everyone seemed very congenial. Following the meeting we were free for the evening.

The couple from Canada invited us to go down town with them. When the four of us exited the cab we found we were among multitudes upon multitudes of people who were crowding the streets. It seemed Saturday night in the Madrid center was a "big thing" for almost everyone living in the city. Some streets were so jammed we chose not to go near them because there didn't seem to be room for one more person. The people pressed from store front, across the pavement, across the street, across the opposite pavement and on up to the other store front.

Within a few blocks we saw two restaurants named "Muslim del jalmon" which looked clean and were filled with customers. Our new found friends Mary and Kevin seemed drawn to the restaurant's window and then the four of us followed our noses inside. The whole place was packed with people. On the second floor we found one table was open and we grabbed it. Once we tasted the food there was no question about why so many people filled the place. The food was very good and a reasonable price.

Our watches showed the time was after nine o'clock by the time we finished eating. We strolled a few more streets to enjoy the night lights and jovial people. Then the four of us determined we were tired and ready for a good nights sleep.

By eight a.m. the next morning 39 people were seated in the Hotel dining room to enjoy their buffet breakfast. There were copious amounts of well-prepared tasty food and with full tummy's we all seated ourselves on the tour bus for a day of adventure.

Just an hour's drive from Madrid came Toledo, the once capital city of Spain and our first stop. First, from a distant bluff, we viewed the impressive sight of the castle, the Cathedral and the surrounding city. Toledo reminded me of Masada in Israel; a city built high on a bluff and well fortified from any attacker. Unlike Masada, Toledo's three bluff sides were protected by a river.

In order for us to reach the city required a strenuous climb, although not as strenuous as it was for people visiting the city several years ago. To encourage tourism some wise city planners installed escalators for the major part of the climb. Even though we rode the escalators there was still a very steep walk for about a quarter of a mile before we reached the square at the center of the city.

Beautiful Toledo Cathedral filled one side of the square. We learned it took 300 years to build the Cathedral and a change in the architecture was noted in the last section built. Across the square from the Cathedral sat another large building to house the Bishop and beside the Bishop's house stood the government building. Everyone in our group kept their camera's ready to capture scene after scene; snap after snap was taken. No one was more busy with their camera than Jessica as she brought with her a multitude of rolls of film to capture every aspect of the trip.

Next we were led down a cobblestone street to a smaller church where one of El Greco's famous paintings hung. It filled one whole wall and was magnificent in color. Several minutes were taken by our guide to explain the stories about the figures in the painting.

Because the painting fit perfectly into the wall we were viewing we were surprised to learn the painting was moved from another wall of the church to the present one in the year 2000. However, when the workmen made the move, they and the parishioners of the church were surprised more than we were because they found the tomb of El Greco behind the wall on which the painting was originally placed.

El Greco's son built the second tower of Toledo's Cathedral. The first tower is quite a bit taller than one the artist's son built. This difference in size was due to the fact the city was running out of money by the last of the 300 years of construction. Despite the smaller size and different design the second tower was very impressive. The son showed extreme talent.

On leaving the church our group went into a jewelry making shop to see how the lovely twenty-four carrot gold designs were made on necklaces, earrings and tie clasps. These seemed ideal items to take home for gifts.

From Toledo the group traveled south through the country where the setting for the novel Don Quixote (by Cervantes) took place. In the distance we saw the actual castle, with the windmills located on each side, as mentioned in the book. Stationed right by the road stood a statue of Don Quixote on his steed with his sidekick on a mule along side of him.

With a four hour bus ride before us we needed to stop to eat lunch at a small cafeteria on the road. The cafeteria owner seemed overwhelmed when such a large volume of people descended upon him.

I ordered an "omelet" sandwich. What I received was a surprise. Evidently the cook prepared a chopped boiled eggs with chopped boiled potatoes combination early in the day and set it in the refrigerator to congeal. Then when the sandwich was ordered he cut the slab mass into wedges and served the wedge on an eight inch hard roll. The best opinion I can give is "The bread was good."

We were on our way to Grenada to spend the night, plus a tour on the next day. Moorish architecture was very evident in the lovely hotel where we stayed. Jessica and I ate our dinner in the hotel dining room while the rest of the group went out to eat at one of the extra options offered to tourists. The two of us did not feel the extra cost of the option was something we wanted to spend. So a delightful dinner (at one quarter of the cost of the one the tour group went to) was enjoyed at the hotel. Jessica sank her teeth into a thick juicy steak while I was very pleased with salmon bathed in a seafood sauce.

Grenada's temperature seemed pleasingly warm, while in the distance snow-capped mountains could be seen. The climate could be classified as semitropical with the occasional cacti growing.

Day three dawned with perfect weather for a walk. And walking, walking, walking filled the entire morning as we toured the Alhambra. This magnificent palace was built for a Sultan during Spain's occupation by the Moors and is the area's main tourist attraction. The buildings have been standing for over 600 years with the ornate rooms kept in as perfect condition as when the Sultan lived there. A Mosque, plus a picturesque pool is located within the palace and beautiful gardens are adjacent to the structure.

Our group left the gardens around noon to travel to Seville. We rode for about an hour and a half before stopping again on the road for lunch at a Cafe. The food proved to be again a sorry surprise. Jessica ordered a hamburger as she thought "what can they do wrong to a hamburger?" The meat turned out to be more like sausage and undercooked. Jessica left half of the sandwich on her plate.

I ordered vegetable soup, plus a roll and received a broth with chopped boiled egg and tiny slivers of chopped pork in it. My opinion again - "The roll tasted good."

Seville came into view around four p.m. As soon as we reached the center of the city the bus stopped for us to tour the Cathedral which at one time was a Mosque. As soon as the Muslims were driven from Spain in the late fourteen hundreds work began to turn the Mosque into a Cathedral. It is the largest Gothic church in the world and awesome to walk through. There are many family Chapels as well as the main sanctuary within the one building. Christopher Columbus' crypt sits in one of the wings.

When we left the Cathedral we walked through one of the ancient sections of the city where homes bordered the old city wall. Then off we rode to the hotel where, as a group, we enjoyed dinner together in the hotel dining room. Eight of us sat at a table and were offered the two choices of appetizer, entree, and dessert (all through Spain every restaurant offered only two choices). Each person at the table where Jessica and I sat ordered the seafood cocktail and we were very happy with our choice. Jessica ordered the salmon and I ordered the veal. Both were unusually prepared and delightful to our taste buds. Offered for dessert was a choice of either custard or fruit. In my opinion the rich and creamy custard was the best choice.

For Jessica and my self day three became a day of relaxation. A day tour, with the extra fee, was offered, but we chose to do our own thing. First on our agenda was to sleep late in order to catch up on all the sleep we missed since leaving the states. Sleep we did and we strolled out of our room around noon to find a bite to eat in a little Cafe.

The country of Spain has grove after grove of trees growing sweet oranges and in the eating places the orange juice is squeezed right before the customers eyes; so sweet and good. To accompany my juice I ordered a berry cheesecake with strawberries, blackberries and raspberries on top. Yum!

In the center of Seville there is a lovely walkway along the river where Jessica and I chose to stroll for several blocks and then turned back. On our return walk Jessica and a classmate from the Kentucky college they both attended caught a glimpse of each other and we each stopped for a few minutes to chat. Who would have thought such a chance meeting possible? Both girls knew the other was traveling to Spain, but neither of them knew the other's itinerary.

While browsing the store windows on the main street Jessica saw a ring she decided to buy as her keepsake from Spain. Then too, she couldn't resist another ring she thought her sister would appreciate.

In just a short while the shops would be closing for the siesta time. We found a place from where e-mails could be sent to let the family know all was going well with grandmom and granddaughter, then returned to the hotel.

Jessica and I both enjoy various table games. With this in mind I brought Skippo cards and cards for another game called School along on the trip. These we played while others dozed the afternoon hours away.

Along with our fellow travelers dinner was spent at a Flamingo Restaurant which quickly filled with several tour groups. When the meal service started the Flamingo dance show began. Colorful costumes and exotic dance steps continued through the appetizer, salad, pork dinner and luscious creamy pastry. This became the perfect ending to a relaxing day.

On day four the bus turned west for a visit to Lisbon, Portugal; a six hour drive. The hours were filled with interesting scenery, from time to time explanations from the guide, conversations with fellow passengers, and again eating lunch at a road side Cafeteria. Once more I ordered vegetable soup and this time was pleasantly surprised with real vegetables and a good broth with a delicious roll. Believe Spain has the best tasting bread in the whole world.

After settling into our hotel rooms seven of us decided to go to the Columbo Mall. We were not too surprised to find the huge Mall similar to those large Malls at home, but we were surprised to find Toys-R-us and other American chain stores.

Dinner for the group was scheduled to be held at a restaurant about an hour's drive from Lisbon. Traffic was terrible and the width of the street where the restaurant was located was just wide enough for the bus and one car (whether parked or moving). If any car was parked more than six inches from the curb there was not enough room for the bus to pass.

The reason for the choice of this particular restaurant was because of the special Fado music and the local folk dancing they offered both during the meal and following it. Fado music is very lyrical and tender and this female singer enhanced the beauty of the song with her mellow voice. Interspersed between the songs the lively folk dancing filled the stage.

Everyone received the same food this evening. A good salad, then fish, green beans, carrots and boiled potatoes. Lastly came a rich chocolate pudding, and for those who wanted it brandy was poured onto the pudding.

When the meal was finished the dance troupe moved from the stage to the dance floor and guest dancing began. A few couples from our group took to the dance floor and then one of the older men in the dance troupe came and asked Jessica if she would dance with him. A few dances later he came and asked me. This was the first time in my life I ever danced in a public place and while I felt awkward I enjoyed it.

First on our agenda for the next morning was a bus tour of Lisbon. We drove by the fortress, through the town squares and on to the water front. Before the bus stopped the guide pointed out the bridge built by the same company who built the Golden Gate bridge and many of the statues, including the huge one of Christ, with outstretched arms, looking out toward the city.

We stopped by the tall Discovery statue and walked along the water front to where the river entered the Atlantic Ocean. Then the guide took us through one of the old, very narrow city streets where people sold fish, or vegetables, in small bins outside of their doors. We found the road was so narrow we needed to crowd into any of the doorways in order for a car to pass. Quickly the morning was over and our last stop was the monastery.

The guide told us a legend about the rooster (the state bird) seen on many woven fabric's in the shops and being sold by street venders. According to the story the Apostle James came to the area of the world now known as Portugal. He died there and many pilgrims would come to the visit the site of his grave.

One day a young man coming on the pilgrimage was invited into a house for a dinner party. While the guests were eating the host found out money was stolen and the young man was accused of the crime. He pleaded not guilty before the judge (who was eating at the dinner) and the judge said we will believe you are not guilty when this cooked bird crows. The bird made a noise and the young man was released.

At noon most of the group went on an optional tour while eight of us remained at the downtown square to browse through the many small shops, plus get a bite to eat. Many beggars approached Jessica and myself in the downtown streets. There was also a man shadowing Jessica which gave her an uncomfortable feeling. He was even waving money at her when the two of us decided it was time to hail a cab and return to the hotel.

Back at the hotel there were six of us who ate dinner together during the evening hours. This was the only place offering more than two choices on the menu. We were all so thankful Jessica could understand the Spanish and tell us what the different items were. She ordered chicken. I ordered lasagna and while my food was prepared differently than it would have been in America, it was tasty.

On the next day miles upon miles stretched before us from the port of Lisbon, Portugal to Salamanca, Spain. For the mid-morning break we stopped at the site of Fatima where we were free to roam the lovely grounds to see a memorial built to the three children who claimed to have seen the virgin Mary, plus other architecture that produced a sense of worship.

In 1917 when the children told their story there was nothing but woods in the isolated area. Today a small town, containing mostly restaurants and religious relic shops, is adjacent to the Fatima site.

There was a story about the virgin giving Fatima a message which she was to keep secret from the public. The message was about an attempt some day on a pope's life. Sixty years later when the attempt to assassinate pope John took place the public heard about the virgin's message and the pope was taken to the Fatima site to recuperate from the bullet wound.

Every year, day after day, many pilgrims come to pray, and on the date of the day of Fatima's visitation there are thousands more who come to the huge square for worship. Two of the three children are buried in a small Chapel where a daily mass takes place.

We spent an hour at this location then rode for two more hours before stopping for lunch. My soup and bread was delicious. Jessica and I could not resist one of the double-dipped ice cream bars. The dark chocolate on top of light chocolate over vanilla ice cream seemed to be a bar we would find very hard to not buy in future days.

Three more hours of travel followed the two o'clock lunch break. All through the day we were riding through woods and mountains with only a few settlements coming into view; very picturesque and pleasurable scenery to watch.

Shortly after checking into the Salamanca hotel a tour was planned to leave at 6:30 p.m.. Darkness was not quite upon us when we approached the town square where lovely ornate, three story high, walls encased the four sides of the square. In the center of each one of the wall's stood an arched entry into the square.

This was Friday evening and being a University town there were hundreds of young people walking through the square and shopping in small shops located in the wall. Many more young people were walking the narrow streets adjacent to the wall where more shops could be found.

The tour took us from the square to the University and then the Cathedral. However both closed their doors to the public at six and we were not allowed inside. Our guide gave us some information while we looked at the interesting old architecture of both buildings. Salamanca University was completed and has been in use since the thirteen hundreds. The Cathedral was completed in the fifteen hundreds.

Jessica and I took advantage of the hour and a half remaining before the dinner hour by strolling two of the busy streets along side of the square.

Thirty-nine people sat around two tables in the hotel dining room to chat and just enjoy being together. In the past week's time we became a close group of friends. The hotel food was good with the choice of either poultry or salmon as the entree. Everyone received vegetable soup as an appetizer, fried potatoes and salad accompanied our meat and there was three flavored ice cream for desert. As after every dinner we returned to our rooms for a night's sleep on a full tummy.

The return to Madrid happened the very next day with leaving Salamanca at eight in the morning and arriving in Madrid at noon. After an hour's drive the bus pulled to the side of the road for us to view a city completely encased in its original Roman wall. The concept was awesome and many of us stepped off the bus to snap pictures.

Being the lunch hour at our Madrid arrival everyone was given free time to grab a bite to eat in the city's core, before going on tour. Jessica and I, plus about a dozen others from the group, went to McDonald's. For some reason the cheese-burger tasted even better to me than those at home. Maybe it was because I had not eaten one for several weeks, or maybe it was because of the extra good Spanish baked roll.

Now to the Prado Museum for a guided tour. Beautiful art work filled our eyes for several hours. Most impressive to me was the work of Goya depicting the three stages of Spanish life; pre-civil war, during the war, and the most grotesque art of the post war period.

Jessica wanted to take one more picture on her eight rolls of film. This was of the soccer stadium located a few blocks from our hotel. There was plenty of time between the museum tour and dinner for us to walk there and return. With soccer being a major sport in this country and an international game taking place this very night a picture of the stadium was appropriate and the picture was snapped.

Days pass quickly when people are enjoying themselves. Most of us could hardly believe this was our last evening together. We were escorted to another quaint restaurant. I went "all-out Spanish" and tasted gaspacho soup for the first time. It was g-o-o-d. Then enjoyed piela, a seafood dish, and for dessert the all American baked Alaska.

Melodious music filled the last half hour with three men singing and accompanying themselves with guitar and mandolin, and so closed the last evening. While meandering back to the hotel the bus took the long way in order for us to see the lovely night lights on fountains, arches, gates and buildings.

Only the long flight home remains for each of us. But there would be days of telling family and friends about the excellent hotels, delicious food and extraordinary sights of Spain and Portugal. There would also be the occasional correspondence between our new found friends and ourselves.

God truly blessed Jessica and myself with our time together. We learned much and enjoyed much. How fortunate we are to be able to hold this holiday time in our memory.

SUITCASE WOES

The plan was to fly from the state of Washington to the nations capital of Wash- into DC. As so often happens - nothing of the air time went as planned. I was listed to depart at 8:50 a.m. on a through flight to the Dulles airport and I arrived at the Seattle, WA. airport at 5:30 a.m.

Surely my eyes were deceiving me to find the check-in line winding along one wall after another to a total of about three blocks. Once I found the end of the line a whole hour was consumed in just reaching the ticket counter to check in my bags and to receive a boarding pass.

The next step was standing in another line to have the bags x-rayed before they would be allowed to go into the hold of the aircraft. Then still one more line waited for me in order to pass through security, and I arrived at the boarding gate to find the area thick with people.

Any prospect of my getting on this flight faded because my hand held a standby ticket. The plane to the Dulles airport was full and I did not get on while my bags did.

The next departure for Washington was at 1 p.m. and once more I was listed to be on the plane; if there was an open seat I would get on. However this flight was bound for the Reagan airport (located close to the center of the city of Washington) instead of the suburban Dulles airport. I did get on the Reagan bound plane and enjoyed a turbulent-free ride, plus a tasty meal.

About an hour before landing the stewardess announced, "If you need to leave your seat do it now. During the last half hour of the flight anyone leaving their seat will cause the plane to be diverted from landing at the Reagan airport." This announcement was repeated every fine minutes and fortunately it was obeyed. We landed at the Reagan airport at 9:30 p.m.

By 10:15 p.m. a rental car was in my possession and I was driving toward the other DC airport. Before leaving home I spent time scanning my Atlas to find where the Dulles airport was located. It was sitting west of the city.

Three times I stopped to ask for specific directions and each time was told, "Oh, the road signs will clearly show you the way." Either the road I was on did not have signs, or else I missed them. By 11:30 p.m. I was still driving and ready to cry because I had been up since 4 a.m. and I could not find something as big as an airport.

Enough was enough! A Best Western Motel came into view and I knew right away it would be my overnight stopping place. Before going to my room the clerk gave me a map with the route to the airport marked. I slept well.

The next morning at the "breakfast included" motel the dining room was full. I sat at a table with three other people; a couple from NY (the gentleman was a fire- fighter) and a single man from North Carolina who in Washington to attend a Christian Conference.

The North Carolina man began to talk about a vision he experienced during the night and described seeing the throne room of God. The man from NY said, "Did you see the Lamb of God?" What a reassurance I felt to be sitting with Christians and because the company was so enjoyable we chatted a long time before parting.

The drive to Dulles took about 45 minutes and I pulled into the parking lot a little after 10 a.m., while thinking, I would arrive at the home where I was scheduled to stay by mid- afternoon. Then there would be plenty of time to relax and also prepare for my three Representations of InterAct Ministries at the coming Sunday morning services.

Boldly I tramp into the airport and up to the baggage security to learn it was only open from 6 a.m. to 9 a.m. and again from 2 p.m. to 10 p.m. Ugh - a four hour wait before I could get my luggage and this meant I wouldn't arrive at my friends home until evening. Russ and Dottie Dokerty held dinner for us to be able to enjoy it together.

The purpose of this trip east was to share the ministry, plus be involved in a family reunion. For three weeks I stayed in Missionary housing in Ventnor, NJ and during the second week a second house was available to sleep the Temple children and grandchildren. There were nine bedrooms used to house 19 people.

We enjoyed a grand time together on the beach, walking the boardwalk, playing games, eating dinner together and eating out. On July fourth one sister-in-law, one brother-in-law and his spouse, plus nieces and nephews (15 in all) joined us for the day and a pot luck dinner. The week will go down in memory as a great one.

During the first and third weeks meetings in Pennsylvania and Maryland I shared at two morning church services, one Sunday School, plus an evening home meeting. Slides of my trip to Siberia were shared in these meetings, plus five more times in my prayer partners homes..

The whole time in New Jersey could receive a plus after plus for blessing after blessing. Actually there was one stressful evening when my daughter Pauline, my granddaughter Krystal and her husband Kyle were supposed to be picked up at the Philadelphia airport. The grandchildren were to arrive at 6 p.m. and my daughter at 8 p.m. When I arrived at 8 p.m. to pick them all up Krystal and Kyle were nowhere in sight. I waited and waited and no Pauline showed up either.

People were sitting and standing everywhere. Many were at the airport monitors to learn their flights were canceled, or else there were late arrivals due to terrible storms. Finally Pauline's plane landed around ten o'clock, but the grandchildren didn't come in until midnight. We pulled into the Ventnor parking lot around 1:30 a.m. and collapsed into bed.

What is there about my entering an airport that I should always expect the unexpected to happen?

TOPMOST TOWN

Hour after hour the airplane droned north and I traveled from colorful fall draped foliage to the land of permafrost where there were no trees. We landed in Barrow, Alaska, 300 miles north of the Arctic circle, a town ten and a half hours travel time north of Seattle, Washington.

The season was early October and off of the Arctic ocean the worst storm in fifty years was just abating. Yes, there was snow on the ground, plus a chilly twenty-nine degrees temperature, but with the warm face of David my son greeting me, plus a kiss and precious hugs the frosty air was dispelled.

David became transplanted from Colorado to the northern-most town upon the north American continent just a few months before my arrival because of a job opportunity with Cape Smythe airlines.

I wasn't in David's home five minutes before he showed me how to load his high powered rifle, plus his magnum hand gun. David needed to be alert and always armed because of the ever present threat of meeting a polar bear (who think people are tasty tidbits). This danger was known to me before ever going to Barrow.

At a very young age my father and brother taught me how to use a gun and I was not afraid to protect myself with one. However going outside alone was not planned to be high on my priority list . When I did go I became a pistol-packing missionary with a magnum in one pocket and a camera in the other.

David's home was right on the beach of the Arctic Ocean and to my surprise it was not frozen in October. When we strolled the shore there were other facts amazing to me. Sitting on the sand were jellyfish, and starfish and other creatures and Eskimos were digging for clams. For some reason any thought of the possibility of such sea life living so far north never seemed likely .

Barrow has a Polar Bear Patrol constantly driving the perimeter of the dwellings for the safety of the 4500 people living there. If a bear is seen walking toward the town the patrolman will shoot over the its head. If the bear keeps coming then it is shot with a tranquilizer and hauled away from the town. There are times though when the animal must be destroyed.

The patrol is not on duty after dark and a bear could come into town during the night causing a resident to possibly find one sleeping their doorstep.

This particular fall there were many bears on land. Usually they come off the ice in the spring to give birth in a denning area. Then return to the ice shortly thereafter to feast on the walrus and seal out on the ice. However, because the wind blew the ice way off shore this year there were many hungry bears on land.

The architecture of the town is one of contrasts. There are old weathered homes and shops which have been in use since the early twentieth century by Eskimos and white settlers. Then there are new buildings; homes, schools, a post office, shopping center and museum, with all being the product of being in a oil rich area.

Several things impressed me concerning the town. One was the friendliness of the residents and another was the sense of Christianity being lived in the lives of the people.

Presbyterian missionaries traveled to this area a hundred years ago. They established a church and a hospital, both of which are still very active. On Sunday I attended the Presbyterian church where there were about 80 Eskimo people, and about a dozen Caucasian ones present. The Pastor is an Eskimo and this particular Sunday one of the elders gave his testimony.

Christian principles were brought into practice in the town's laws. For example, during the time when many whaling ships came into Barrow they brought liquor with them. The Eskimo people became constantly drunk. There were murders, suicides and the people's every day needs were not met. Men under the influence held no desire to hunt or fish, therefore there was no food on the table.

When the Christians became aware of how the people were being destroyed by alcohol they met with the town council to determine what should be done. Their decision was to hold a town meeting with the objective to discuss what was happening and bring to a vote whether the town would stay wet, or become dry.

The vote was to become dry, with a clause as to the vote being taken again every year. Later the vote became a three-way choice; wet, dry, or damp. Damp being alcohol could be used in the home, but it could not be purchased anywhere in town. This of course meant the drink could only be purchased hundreds of miles south and brought by plane or boat to their home.

There were times when David's phone would ring because a friend noted a polar bear was walking close to where they lived. Then he would say, "Come on mother, we'll go see a bear", and we would jump into his vehicle to drive where the animal could be watched. Usually the bear would be out walking on a frozen lagoon, or sunning itself on the beach. Of course we would not get out of the car.

One evening the telephone rang for the caller to announce, "A whale had been caught." This time David and I joined a caravan of vehicles on their way to see the catch brought in.

The International Ocean Management Bureau has allotted Barrow twelve whales a year to harvest. When one is caught it is cause for a big celebration as the meat becomes distributed to all of the town's residents and Muktuk (Whale) is the customary Thanksgiving and Christmas dinner this far north.

Fishermen go out in small boats. After a whale is located and harpooned it is towed up to the beach by a rope attached to the tail.

As the evening sun was setting I saw the boat with the whale about 100 feet from shore. On the beach sat a huge earth-moving machine ready to bring the huge creature up onto the gravel-like sand.

Many people were gathered around to congratulate the captain and admire the catch. It must have been 25 feet long and the body about five feet thick. Within 20 minutes the carving began from the backbone down to the middle of the abdomen. Strips about 18 inches wide and ten inches thick were pulled-off and laid side-by-side for the captain and crew to have first choice. Then the other families would get a share.

When all of the meat was removed the huge carcass was hauled a distance from town for the polar bears to feast on. Only the immense head bone remained when the bears were finished.

Families hauled the meat home and left it outside to stay frozen until they were ready to use it.

Ten days flew by quickly and the Sunday before I was to leave David drove me (after church) out to Barrow Community College because the school's dining room offers a Buffet Brunch open to the public on this day of the week. The school is located just past the eastern edge of town. An area we were close to several times while watching the bears.

Almost at the school property we saw a man walking along the side of the road. David stopped and asked him, "Are you armed?" The man had a puzzled look on his face and replied, "No." David said, "Do you know there is the possibility of running into a polar bear around here." His answer was, "Yes I heard announced on the radio they were here."

My son said, "You should really get in the car," and the gentleman did. We learned he was from Holland and had only been in town a few days. The concept of the radio making bear announcements to warn people to not go into the area unless protected never entered the man's head.

After eating a tasty meal at the College we drove the man a short distance where David and I saw a bear the day before. There were two out on the lagoon and from the car the three of us watched their movements.

On my flight south many interesting pleasant memories kept surfacing. I knew I'd be ready to visit Barrow again at any time.

PLANES AND BUSES

The purpose of the trip was to Represent InterAct Ministries in churches and at a Christian College Conference in Kentucky, Mississippi and Alabama. Things went smoothly for two weeks; good meetings and a good Conference. Then interesting, or unusual, or unexpected things began to happen.

From Lexington, Ky. south to more rural towns the most sensible and economical way to travel is by bus. I should have known things were going to be different when I learned I was routed north to go south. I traveled From Lexington, KY, north to Cincinnati, Oh., then southwest to Louisville, Ky., on south to Memphis, TN. and lastly south to Oxford, MS; bringing about a fifteen hour overnight ride.

Fortunately two seats were open and I was able to stretch out and catnap most of the night. When occasionally waking I saw falling snow and sleet being flipped off the windshield by the wipers. A sense of possible danger came to mind, but also a relief over not driving a rental car through the mess by myself.

Little did I know I would be in a hospital ICU waiting area two hours after arrival in Oxford, but there I landed. No, not as a patient, but to accompany my friend Ann Lewis who works as a volunteer at the unit on Thursday mornings. The room was filled with hurting family members of people sick in intensive care.

172

Ann's job was to answer the phone and answer questions of people in the room, plus keep the coffee pot always filled. I chatted with Ann, chatted with the anxious people, straightened magazines laying on tables and answered the phone when Ann could not.

InterAct Ministries motto is, "Expect the unexpected." Well, this was sure one unexpected experience for me. A few hours later Ann and I were with her Senior's church group for an afternoon of social fellowship. Then the following evening I showed my Siberian slides in Ann and her sister Julia's home.

Early Saturday morning another long bus ride lay before me; leaving Oxford, MS. at 7:40 a.m. and supposedly arriving in Selma, AL. at 6:30 p.m. Two bus changes were in the schedule. One in Birmingham, AL and the other in Montgomery, AL.

Morning hours went smoothly and then when I landed in Birmingham I learned my connecting bus would be two hours late. Of course this meant the bus change in Montgomery would be missed. Now I'd be arriving in Selma, AL at 10:30 p.m.

Several hours of people watching took place in Birmingham. Some were short and some were tall. Some were skinny and some were heavy. Every possible shade of skin sat, or walked through the terminal during this time.

One young black woman I particularly noticed was tall and heavy. It was not her size which caught my attention, but the fact both of her hands were wrapped in gauze. She held them at her waist and a little extended from her body.

About a half hour before I was to board my bus I was just about ready to leave the ladies room when out of one of the stalls came the lady with the wrapped hands. She looked at me and said, "Please have pity on me." The poor woman could not pull up her underwear or slacks.

For a few minutes I wrestled with her clothing while trying to get everything in place. The next thing I knew I was wrapped in a big bear hug and heard, "God Bless You!" She told me a metal bar had fallen on her hands and broken both of them. At this time I had no idea how precious her blessing would be to me.

Vaguely, I remembered the name Selma, AL in the past news, but I did not remember what brought it into the news. I was going to be stepping off the bus at 10:30 at night in the downtown core of this town.

The next day I learned Selma was the center of the Black Muslim movement. A group of people who believe white people are the children of Satan. My skin was definitely the wrong color for this area. For Selma and a few other southern places I definitely needed the blessing given to me in the ladies room.

A dear Pastor met the bus and for the next day and a half sweet fellowship took place in a church about a half hour south of Selma. God blessed during the InterAct Ministries presentation and dear people tried to fill my every need.

Before I knew it I was back on the bus headed to Montgomery and then Atlanta, GA. My ticket said I would travel from Atlanta to Lexington, KY. There was nothing about bus changes in Nashville, TN. Louisville, KY and Cincinnati, OH before reaching Lexington. To top this crazy schedule was the fact the bus I was to take in Atlanta was late, and of course this changed every bus transfer. Originally I was to arrive in Lexington at 8 a.m. on Tuesday morning. Not possible - my bus pulled into the Lexington terminal at 2:30 p.m.

The late schedule was endurable, but the hatred I felt was excruciating. The same hatred I felt in the town of Selma sat on many faces in southern bus terminals. People looked at me like I was scum. One lady who sat next to me on one of the buses tried to make me feel as uncomfortable as possible by constantly pushing me into the side of the bus.

Once back in Lexington pleasure followed the hours of discomfort. After a good night's sleep there followed the fun of celebrating Valentines Day plus a birthday dinner for my son. It had not been my pleasure to be with them for these events for quite a few years.

Kentucky experienced much ice and snow for most of February. The day before I was to fly home one of the worst ice storms in years hit. First there were hours of freezing rain. Every twig, branch and tree trunk were covered with thick ice. Many power lines came down and thousands of homes were without electricity.

When my flight time arrived for traveling back west the airport was open. But planes were late arriving and after taking the time to deice before takeoff they were very late leaving.

Seems like my air schedule was becoming as bad as the bus schedule. I was to change planes in Detroit and the flight I was on landed about the same time my connecting flight took off.

There were no other flights to Seattle this night and I was stranded at the airport. I wasn't alone as several other people were stranded due to the weather. They sat in clumps here and there in waiting areas. I joined one of the clumps of ladies.

We pulled a row of chairs close to us so we could put our feet up, then scrunched our bodies down in the chairs we were sitting on. Sleep over came us one by one.

After about two hours I woke with a start. There was the sensation something was covering me. An uncomfortable feeling filled me until I saw it was a blanket. Some airline employee cared enough to go around to all the sleeping people and cover them with a blanket.

Was the trip worth while? The answer is definitely "yes." There were hardships, but there was also the joy of sharing the ministry, and being with family, plus constant reminders of God's love. Seems difficulties become unimportant where there are people who care enough to show they care.

ITALY'S HIGHLIGHTS

For two years Pauline and I waited. Yes, this is the trip we were supposed to have taken on 9-11.

Seattle to Rome Italy takes many flying hours with little sleep and we wondered how we ever would have enough energy to go on a three hour walking tour once we landed there. The surprise to us was there was no problem. Maybe it was because of the excitement of being in the city of Rome where the apostles Peter and Paul spent the last days of their lives.

Thirty-two people gathered together to meet for the first time in one of Rome's Hotel lobbies to be briefed on what we would see and do for the next 24 hours in the city. Lorenzo was the name of the guide who gave the briefing. He seemed to be a gentleman with wit and knowledge. We found out he has been leading tours for the past 48 years of his life.

One hour after the briefing a comfortable bus carried us off to see Rome's ancient buildings, fountains and the city's night lighting.

Many things stand out in my mind from this evening. Among them walking along buildings used by Romans which were still in use. Then there was The Pantheon and the Four Continents Fountain. We walked up very thin steps where chariots once ascended in order for the drivers to go into government buildings at the top of the hill. However the most impressive sight to the eyes this night was the lighting on the Forum ruins. Time was given for everyone to have dinner on their own. Pauline and I found a quiet little restaurant close to the Pantheon with a sign saying their special for the evening was Ziti. We sat at one of the out door tables and ordered the special; it was delicious and we felt full. Upon getting ready to leave out comes the waiter with plates of eggplant parmesan for us and we were introduced to the large meals served in Italy. Once more both of us thought we would leave when we learned the superb Italian gelati dessert would end our meal. Lemon and strawberry gelati tickled our taste buds and our stomachs kept crying, "no more, no more."

The whole evening proved enjoyable and became just a little foretaste of the whirlwind tour to enfold before us.

Early the next morning 32 strangers entered the bus to become close friends as the days progressed.

Our group was the second in line to enter the Vatican museum. While we waited there for the doors to open tour bus after tour bus stopped to spit-out their contents. The entry line became longer and longer.

Many carved Roman works of art filled the first part of the museum. Then came other pieces of stonework commissioned by the Pope. A slight disappointment followed when we found out the tapestry gallery was closed for repairs. However our feet next stepped into the Sistine Chapel and we saw beauty beyond words. Pauline and I stood and gawked at the wonder of the walls and ceiling; such perfect features, such realistic color and beauty was almost beyond comprehension.

The day of awe was just beginning as our guide next took us into St. Peter's Basilica, the largest Gothic Church in the world. Not only can it claim to being the largest it can also revel in the beauty and artwork contained within.

The Pieta was off to one side and encased in glass. In a sense the viewing of it here was a disappointment to me. My mind well remembered the breathtaking beauty of the Pieta in the darkened room at the New York World's Fair. There one spotlight focused on the marble beauty and peoples eyes couldn't help but rivet on Mary holding her thirty-three old Son.

Of course not too long ago some deranged person attempted to destroy the Pieta in St. Peter's church and the placement of the statue behind bulletproof glass is understandable, but a shame it has to be that way.

Time was flying bye and most of us were now hungry. We ate lunch in a restaurant along side of St. Peter's church. Then boarded the bus for another section of Rome to see the Coliseum where Roman gladiators fought. Several of us walked around the Capotine Hill and on to the Forum. As the sun crept well toward the west the last stop for this day was a visit to the Catacombs.

Most of the people in our group were well aware of the stories told about Christians hiding in the Catacombs. The tour guide refuted this belief and told us this was not true. He claimed the place was only a cemetery where thousands of Christians were buried, but no Christian ever hid there.

Walking through the dark narrow recesses, seeing burial spot after burial spot, heartache filled me and I still hung to the belief that Christians hid there. It was a perfect place for dear ones who needed to hide from Rome's cruelty. The dimly lit tunnels went on for miles after miles.

A short rest was scheduled back at the hotel before we traveled to a fine restaurant for a late dinner. The romantic-looking place sat on a hill from where night views of Rome could be seen.

Course after course of delicious food was served and we ate and ate and ate. The typically Italian low alcohol content wine was free and I tasted both the white and red varieties. However, according to my taste buds there isn't a wine I've yet found I would like to drink.

Music began, but dancing did not seem a priority for the majority of the couples (Pauline and I were the only singles). The tour director came to Pauline and asked her to dance, but she refused. Then he came to me and asked me to dance. I declined but he kept insisting and I finally joined him. This was the fourth time in my life I danced with a man (twice before with a son and the other time while being in Spain).

Not being exactly sure how to dance I found the step was mostly just swaying side to side and no problem seemed to come. Two more gentlemen asked me to dance and again I managed to not trip any of them.

I did not learn to dance as a teenager because my father thought it was sinful. Then too, as a young person my life was filled ice skating and swimming and basketball and church activities, plus being very involved with music, so there never seemed time to go to dances. My hubby claimed he had two left feet and would not attempt to learn to dance. Dancing at this stage of my life seemed like it could be fun.

Following the dinner the bus took us to the Fountain of Trevi where we threw coins into it while acting out the movie's song. From this fountain we walked to the Spanish steps and then on to see more of the night lights. Everyone was well ready for bed by now and we collapsed once we reached them.

Lorenzo believed in early starts. Our first day of bus travel began right after breakfast. We were on our way to Florence, with one stop at the town of Siena. While traveling on the bus our guide told us about the importance of the saintly objects to Italian people. To them there was not a greater relic than the actual body of a saint. Lorenzo finished the explanation with the story of a saintly woman who was born in one town and who died in another town. Both towns argued over who was to keep the body until the decision came to dismember the head from the body. The head would be placed in the Cathedral in Siena while the body would be placed in the other town.

The first place we visited in Siena was the Cathedral and just as Lorenzo said the head was on display in front of the altar.

Upon coming out of the Cathedral the noon hour rang. Because all of us in the group were hungry we walked down to the town square where we found many shops to browse and places to eat sitting along the square. Pauline and my mouths were watering to try some true Italian pizza. Of course there followed the action of entering the first shop advertising it and found there could be no other description of the crust, sauce, cheese and meat but delicious.

In another hour the bus began traveling toward Florence. Our guide became eloquent on the sculpture, painting and architectural gifts of Michaelangelo. Lorenzo said, "Michaelangelo most enjoyed working on sculpture. However several times when Michaelangelo would start working on a sculpture he would be contacted by the Pope to come work on some painting this head of the church wanted done. Michaelangelo would leave what he was working on to do the Pope's bidding."

First on our Florence agenda was a visit to the Cathedral where several of Michaelangelo's half-finished carvings were on display. They were unique, but the most impressive object in this building was the finished statue of David.

Next we walked to the town square to see many more pieces sculpture by other artists filling the portico's around the square. Along the way we stepped into the beautiful Holy Cross Church.

A trip to Pisa was made from Florence. For some reason I always imagined the famed tower stood alone. To my surprise a huge Cathedral sat before the tower and in front of the Cathedral sat another immense edifice used solely for baptisms. Truly the tower does lean quite a bit and in a certain position people can stand where when a picture is taken it seems they are holding the tower up. Of course this action needed to be captured by camera carrying tourists before any of us could move on.

By late afternoon we were back to Florence and touring a famous leather making shop where we watched gold being worked into the leather. Many of us bought leather objects for family gifts and we were able to have the gift recipient's initials imbedded in gold into the leather.

Still some time remained before dinner at the hotel. Many of us browsed other shops close to the leather one.

For the next day the travel plan took us to Verona and Venice. Our stop in Verona was just for a short while. First to view the Roman area, then walk by the balcony proposed to be where Romeo and Juliet courted. Time was taken to eat lunch and then we boarded the bus again.

Venice stands out in my mind as an extremely interesting city. To reach our hotel we traveled by boat and to reach the center of town another launch trip was necessary.

By the town square where St. Mark's Basilica stood there were gondolas ready to carry us through the many canals. To see homes and apartment buildings with a water entrance seemed intriguing. Small craft were parked by the entryways to where the people lived. Many gondolas filled with people were on the water and some of the gondoliers entertained their passengers by singing. Following the "water taxi" ride Lorenzo took us to a glass blowing factory where we watched the process of various shapes being formed After the demonstration some time was spent in the salesroom just enjoying the beauty of the craft and for those interested in doing so to make purchases.

The next morning was free for everyone to spend time looking whereever they wanted. First Pauline and I went into the Byzantine Basilica and found an exquisite place of worship filled with artifacts. Then on into the huge fascinating Doges Palace where in room after room sat beautiful antique furniture. The palace was immense and connected to an ancient prison. The two of us spent the entire morning just looking and looking.

For the lunch hour a small launch took us out into the lagoon to one of the little islands close to Venice. The first sight to strike our eyes were vividly colored homes. Lorenzo told us each color represented a family name and the people painted their houses their name color. Down the town's canal were brilliant red, green, blue, yellow and purple houses.

While the island was small the lunch they served there was NOT small; twelve Courses were placed in front of us. We ate pate, salad, bread, seafood lasagna, fish, shrimp, calamari, fruit, custard and on and on.

Following the lunch Pauline and I walked along the canal for a while and then into a lace-making shop where we observed a woman stitching on a doily. The shopkeeper told us each piece contained seven different stitches. Woman learned one stitch therefore it would take seven women to make one doily, or a scarf, or whatever object wanted. The ladies worked one after another and they used silk thread; a specialty of this island's lace making. The work was exceptionally beautiful, so of course Pauline and I couldn't resist purchasing one of the doilies.

For some reason dinner did not seem as important this evening, even though the food was tasty. Could it have been the extremely large lunch which dulled our appetites?

On day eight's departure from Venice to Assisi the ride was through thick morning fog. Lorenzo assured us the view along the Adriatic coast was spectacular, but we were never able to see it.

Our midday stop was in the Roman town of Ravenna where another Byzantine Cathedral stood. Here one mosaic after another caught our attention with the most fantastic one being made of beaten gold and sitting in front of the altar. The work stood approximately five feet by three feet and consisted of one small square after another with a figure beaten into the center of each one of them. We were told the entire work took four hundred years to complete.

By late afternoon the town of Assisi perched high on Mt. Subasio could be seen in the distance. There was no way far a bus to make an assent up the steep, narrow road and we filed into vans to climb the hill side. From the top the view over the valley was magnificent and a extra bonus was our hotel faced the valley.

This was the only lodging on the trip where Pauline and I were in separate rooms. Actually the size of our rooms reminded me of a monk's cell, but they were clean and there was a tiny bath in what once must have been the room's closet.

The room's size did not matter because at one end there were double doors opening out onto a verandah from where the magnificent view of the valley stretched beyond. This compensated for any small room.

Of course visiting Assisi would not be complete without a tour of the huge magnificent St. Frances Basilica. Then we were free to browse shops and another lovely Cathedral.

Before going to dinner several of us gathered onto the verandah to watch a spectacular sunset. The hotel room where dinner was served reminded me of a twelfth century castle dining hall and the food served there tasted exceptionally good.

Our exciting tour continued south toward the objective being the seaport of Naples in order to board a jet foil with the next destination being Capri. The ride was made with clear skies and breath taking coastal views. Along the way Lorenzo pointed out where the World War II Maginot line extended across southern Italy. One of the men in the tour group was in the U.S. army and served at the Maginot line.

Lorenzo told us the city of Naples was not recommended for tour groups to visit due to an exceptionally high crime rate. The bus took us directly to the dock where there was a little free time to purchase some lunch and we then board the boat.

The town of Capri sits just as high in the air as Assisi does. Therefore small vans were used to transport us from the dock up to the town. Even in the van the ascent and decent were hair-raising experiences because of the narrowness of a road containing one hairpin curve after another. There was hardly room for one vehicle to pass the other and this caused much maneuvering to get by. When ever an oncoming van was seen approaching everyone held their breath because of our consciousness about there being no guard rail and beyond the edge of the road lay a horrific chasm to the water many feet below.

On the top of this hill (jutting straight up out of the bay) sat lovely homes, fantastic views and interesting shops where we spent several hours just looking with our guide often pointing out one special water sight after another. After several hours in Capri we again boarded the boat for a ride to the town of Sorrento, our night's destination.

Now the fact dawned on us that there was only one more day to sight-see in Italy. An entire week was past history. Every day was very fully packed with places and sights and experiences. Usually when traveling I try to keep a daily journal, but this trip was so busy there did not seem to be any time to do this. Now I tried to gather my thoughts as to where I went and where I saw what and where I did what. Getting everything straight would take a little time. The next evening we would be back in Rome.

In the distance from Sorrento could be seen Mt. Vesuvius and Pompeii was our destination for the following morning.

Pompeii lay just a she did before being covered in Ash. After Vesuvius blew almost two centuries passed before archeologists could locate the ancient city and the forty feet of ash could be removed. We walked the narrow streets and lanes. Went into homes, gardens and shops. Saw some of the artwork on walls and found floors with ceramic tile designs. There was even a bakery with a large oven located outside ready to be fired up for use.

Through visiting this city the senses I most felt were ones of destruction and loss of life. People hopelessly killed. We were told ninety percent of the residents fled when the mountain started to rumble. Only ten percent perished because they didn't want to leave their place of business, or they thought they weren't in danger.

As a Christian, thinking of the deeper implication of eternal safety from destruction, Pompeii presents a perfect picture of the false hope people have without knowing Christ.

More beautiful coastal scenes greeted our eyes on the ride north to Rome. The tour was to end this evening with a delicious dinner and lovely concert.

Droning away on the plane home many thoughts filled my mind. I could not name one place I enjoyed more than the other than another; every place held a unique beauty or interest. The Food of Italy can be best described as "yummy", with great quantities and many courses. Here pasta was just one of the courses, not the main course like at home. And pastries are "out of this world."

I thought about one afternoon when Pauline and I were on our own for lunch we went into a bakery to enjoy a substantial meal of just three pastries; a chocolate one, a cinnamon one and one other.

This lunch was on the same day I found my pocket had been picked. When abroad I keep the main quantity of money in a holder under my clothes and just enough money in my zippered jacket pocket to buy lunch and possibly make a few purchases. On this particular day all of my five, ten and twenty euros were already used, so I put a fifty euro in my pocket. To my surprise when I went to pay for lunch the pocket was empty

Friendliness could be the motto of our group. We traveled together, walked together at sites, ate together and told stories about ourselves. Appreciation grew and grew for each person. E-mail addresses were given and some of us have kept in touch since our delightful days in Italy.

QUESTIONS

"Why are you living in Canada when you are an American, is a question repeatedly asked of me. The answer goes back to thirty years ago.

One Sunday evening a missionary came to speak at the church where my husband Chuck, our four children and I attended. He told about the beginning of a new ministry among the North American Indians living in Canada. In the planning stages was the construction of a high school and a Bible School for Christian natives, with the purpose being to prepare them to minister to their own people. The man spoke of a need for teachers and dorm parents. I was a teacher and it seemed the Lord was saying to me "This is where I want you."

On the way home from church I asked Chuck what he thought of the message and the answer was, "Oh, it was all right." There appeared to be no indication the Lord was touching his heart. I did not want to influence my husband on such an important matter, but wanted only the Lord to influence him, so did not tell him I felt called. Instead I asked the Lord how I should pray to find out if He wanted us on the mission field. The idea came to pray, "Lord, if you want us on the mission field make my husband dissatisfied at work." I prayed it daily.

Chuck held a good position at the Boeing Aircraft Company. His hours and salary were comfortable, but God now began impressing on Chuck's mind a Bible verse concerning work and reward. My husband felt he was doing too little work for what he was being paid and asked for more work from his supervisor.

In a few months Boeing went into one of their periodical slumps and many employees were laid off. Chuck was not laid off. However his salary was decreased, but not his workload. This over a period of time was increased to a twelve hour, seven day a week schedule. Then he was transferred to another plant which entailed a one hour drive each way. Chuck left home at four a.m. and returned for supper at six p.m. every day.

In six month's time Chuck became physically and emotionally exhausted. He wasn't able to enjoy family life, or church life and was becoming spiritually starved. From all appearances my dear husband was headed for a nervous breakdown.

The Boeing doctor recommended to Chuck that he take a few days off. We went camping. It was at this time he asked me, "What's going on?" and I told him how daily the Lord was petitioned to make him dissatisfied at work if we were to go to a mission field. Chuck's response was, "Well, if the Lord wants us on the mission field we better find out where He wants us.

Later that day we sat around the campfire with our children, Pauline, Patti, Charles and David (ages 14 to 20) and told them how we felt the Lord was leading us. They each said, "If God wants us on the mission field that is where I want to be."

Next came the job of finding just where we should go. Applications were sent to four ministries; three were mission schools and one was with an evangelist. We wanted to specifically know, so decided to pray for the Lord to reveal His answer through the ministries response to us. They were to tell us there were openings to fit both of our abilities.

The answers came. One mission school only needed one teacher. One school never responded. The evangelist could only use a person with business ability. Three "no" answers! The fourth mission stated they could use us as dorm parents as well as Chuck's business knowledge and my teaching qualifications. We knew where God wanted us to go. It was with the very mission whose representative spoke at our church.

At the end of May, after working for Boeing one month short of twenty years, Chuck resigned. Our family of six moved to a remote area of British Colombia to live in a two room trapper's cabin with no running water or electricity. We cooked by wood and heated the cabin the same way. Each of us were involved in some way with the construction of the school for the summer.

Pauline, Patti and I cooked many a meal on the wood stove to feed the church groups who came to help with the building project. Breakfast, lunch and dinner were served to anywhere between a dozen people to twenty-five people.

Charles and David helped their dad with the actual construction from early morning until the sun went down at eleven p.m. All of the work was of log construction. This style was used in order for our students to feel more at home, because many reserve (reservation) homes were made of logs. The summer's goal was to complete all of the outside construction of two homes, plus a classroom building and the goal was met.

Toward the end of August Chuck needed to go through a legal process to obtain a landed immigrant status in order for our family to live and work in Canada. He drove a hundred miles to the closest city and met with an official to take a three part examination. Points were given for age, for schooling and job type. Chuck was over the age limit they preferred. His schooling was fine, but after pulling out a huge book of job classifications the official could find no similarity between the supervisor's job at Boeing and that of Parish worker, which was the status a missionary held in Canada. The official flunked Chuck and told him he needed to get out of the country within twenty four hours.

What had gone wrong? How could this happen? Why God, why? Were our prayers not answered? For months everything indicated this was where God wanted us and we still believed it. We would not give up yet.

Chuck left the country and then we reapplied through Ottawa. Five months later we were informed there was to be another official interview. Both girls were away at college when Chuck, the boys and I drove to the border for the meeting. We prayed all of the hundred and fifty miles distance driven.

We were not the only ones praying, but extended family members, friends, plus the congregation of our sending church; all of them were praying concerning the customs appointment. Many prayer warriors were beseeching the Lord concerning the outcome of this morning's meeting.

Once more the point system was applied to Chuck's background. Then we were asked to wait outside while the official made his decision. In fifteen minutes we were again called into the office where the official stated, "I have reviewed your case and you do not have enough points to come into Canada." He stopped speaking. We held our breath. Then he went on, "But I have the authority to overrule this decision and I believe you will be a benefit to our country, so you are granted Landed Immigrant status."

Now, how could we ever doubt where God wanted us to be. Three times we prayed. Three times the Sovereign God answered. Impossible odds were overcome and wonderful opportunities were before us. We were on the mission field.

Years have passed since that interview. Our children are all grown and living in the States. My husband, whom the Lord sent to labor for twenty-four years among the North American Indians in Canada, is now with the Lord. I alone am left and still being asked by both Americans and Canadians, "Why are you living in Canada when you are an American?" The only answers I can give is, 1. "Because God sent me." 2. "Because the Almighty still has work for me to do in this northern land."

Dr. June M. Temple

COME TRAVELING WITH JUNE

Художник *С. Журий*
Компьютерная верстка *Д. Рамазанова*

TO ORDER BOOKS

in Canada

Centre for World Mission
Box 2436
Abbotsford, B.C. V2T 4X3

in the United States

Dick Renich
ACW Press Distribution
5501 N. 7th Ave. #502
Phoenix, AZ 85013 - 1755

or

Faith Works / NBN
15200 Faith Works / NBN Way
Blue Ridge Summit, PA 19214

ЛР № 01234 от 17.03.2000
Подписано в печать 27.10.2003. Формат 84x108 $^1/_{32}$.
Бумага офсетная. Гарнитура Нимбусроман. -
Печать офсетная. Усл. печ. л. 20,16
Тираж 1000 экз. Заказ 1290

Миссия евангельских христиан «Шандал»
197198, Россия, Санкт-Петербург, а/я 614
E-mail: mission@shandal.ru; sale@shandal.ru
www.shandal.ru

Отпечатано с готовых диапозитивов
в Академической типографии «Наука» РАН
199034, Санкт-Петербург, 9 линия, 12